ARMS OVER DIPLOMACY

ARMS OVER DIPLOMACY

Reflections on the Persian Gulf War

DENNIS MENOS

PRAEGER

Westport, Connecticut
London

Library of Congress Cataloging-in-Publication Data

Menos, Dennis.
    Arms over diplomacy : reflections on the Persian Gulf War / Dennis
Menos.
      p.   cm.
    Includes bibliographical references (p.   ) and index.
    ISBN 0-275-94160-4 (alk. paper)
    1. Persian Gulf War, 1991—Miscellanea.   I. Title.
DS79.72.M46 1992
955.704'3—dc20   91-44450

British Library Cataloguing in Publication Data is available.

Copyright © 1992 by Dennis Menos

Library of Congress Catalog Card Number: 91-44450
ISBN: 0-275-94160-4

First published in 1992

Praeger Publishers, 88 Post Road West, Westport, CT 06881
An imprint of Greenwood Publishing Group, Inc.

Printed in the United States of America

∞™

The paper used in this book complies with the
Permanent Paper Standard issued by the National
Information Standards Organization (Z39.48-1984).

10 9 8 7 6 5 4 3 2 1

TO DIPLOMACY:

the rational means for settling international disputes

Contents

Preface

The war against Saddam Hussein's Iraq will probably be recorded in history as one of the most popular wars ever fought by the United States. For reasons of national pride, more so than morality, the vast majority of Americans supported the war effort and approved of the President's diplomatic and military moves, which ultimately resulted in Iraq's crushing defeat.

Not all Americans, of course, agreed with the President's handling of the Kuwait crisis. Millions opposed U.S. military involvement in a strange land 7,000 miles away, wondering what possible good could come out of the war and why diplomacy was not being given a chance to resolve the issue peacefully.

Although the speedy and low-casualty outcome of the war has muted much of its active opposition, many Americans still remain troubled over their government's rush to arms in the Gulf, the tragic loss of life on both sides (especially during the closing days of the ground campaign), and the many uncertainties that now confront the United States in the aftermath of its military involvement in the area.

In the euphoria of patriotism and national pride that followed the President's decision to dispatch U.S. forces to the Gulf, opponents of the U.S. involvement were castigated for "not supporting" the troops and for "siding" with Saddam. The charges had nothing to do with the truth, but in a nation anxious to dispel the Vietnam syndrome they proved successful in restraining the opposition to the war and in increasing the President's standing in the polls. With the start of fighting, on January 17, 1991, all open opposition to the war essentially ceased.

It was ludicrous, of course, to charge that persons opposed to the war did not support the troops or that they sided with Saddam. Their argument was not with the troops deployed in Saudi Arabia but rather with the President, who in their judgment was leading the United States in an unjust and immoral war of unknown duration and consequences. As for Saddam Hussein, most Americans were well aware of his repressive regime, his use of chemical weapons against his own people, and his aggression against his neighbors. The Iraqi leader's record of cruelty at home and abroad left him few friends in the United States.

Opposition to the war in the United States was driven by a great many uncertainties and fears, ranging from the propriety of America becoming the "policeman" of the world to the impact on Middle East oil of a protracted conflict to the rationale of the United States shouldering the enormous costs of yet another foreign adventure amidst the many unfulfilled needs at home. As genuine as these and other concerns were, two issues on the agenda of the opposition predominated: concern that the U.S. forces would suffer heavy losses, especially if the war degenerated into a prolonged ground campaign; and apprehension that the United States was becoming increasingly more involved in the quagmire of Middle East politics and its underlying territorial, religious, and security disputes.

It is much too early to judge whether the fears and concerns of the war's opponents were truly justified. Some of their predictions have come to pass; others have not. The final balance sheet on the war cannot be developed until information now held in Washington and Baghdad becomes available on how the crisis would have played had both parties to the dispute elected to follow the route of diplomacy rather than war.

This book contains the reflections of one who was troubled by the administration's decision to go to war against Iraq for the purpose of freeing Kuwait and by the aftereffects of the conflict. The reflections are presented in the form of brief essays, each on a different war issue, and include texts written while the fighting was still in progress and others completed after the war's end. The early essays, those written during the air campaign, are reproduced here as originally written, to include fears that never materialized, views that later were proven wrong, and opinions that in retrospect were invalid. But by reading these essays in their original form, the reader will be able to gain a better appreciation of the emotions, beliefs, and feelings of persons opposed to the war and an understanding of their position.

The book consists of six chapters of text, several appendixes containing key excerpts or summaries from selected documents of the period, a chronology of the war, and a bibliography of the more recent works on the subject. The first two chapters of the text were written while the war was still ongoing. All others were prepared subsequent to the cease-fire ordered by the President on February 27, 1991. They continue to document the author's apprehensions over this entire episode in U.S. history and its likely adverse effect on America's future role in this vital part of the world.

Through the ages, history has been written by the victors of war. Dozens of authors across our land and overseas are probably, at this moment, preparing detailed accounts of the U.S. victory over Iraq. These accounts will be incomplete without an understanding of the views and feelings of the millions of Americans who considered the war over Kuwait to be unnecessary, unjust, and immoral, and one that could have been prevented by better intelligence and more skillful diplomacy.

ARMS OVER DIPLOMACY

1 The Failure of Diplomacy

January 9, 1991

BOTH SIDES MISCALCULATED

U.S. Secretary of State James Baker and Iraqi Minister for Foreign Affairs Tariq Aziz met today for over six hours in Geneva in what has been referred to as the "last chance" for peace. The talks failed to break the diplomatic impasse. Iraq remains determined not to relinquish Kuwait and continues to demand a settlement of the broader Middle East issues, especially that of a Palestinian homeland. The United States insists on unconditional Iraqi compliance with all applicable U.N. resolutions (see Appendix A), including the one calling for Iraq's withdrawal from Kuwait. Any linkage to the Palestinian problem, it asserts, would be "appeasement." Reportedly, France, the Secretary General of the United Nations, Algeria, and others are now prepared to float their own peace initiatives.

The President's Options

Secretary of State Baker asserts that Saddam Hussein miscalculated badly in his handling of the Gulf crisis. The Iraqi leader simply refuses to believe that the United States is serious in its demands for an Iraqi withdrawal from Kuwait or that it is prepared to use military force against him if he ignores the U.N.-imposed deadline of January 15. Iraq is confronting a war with the United States, says Secretary

Baker, because of serious miscalculations by its leader.

Considering the gloom prevailing in the White House as the January 15 deadline approaches, it is obvious that Washington, too, has miscalculated. The United States assumed that assembling a coalition of nations opposed to Iraq's invasion of Kuwait and deploying an armada of men and ships in the area would frighten Saddam Hussein into submission. Had Washington considered the possibility of an unyielding Saddam, its policies would have been much more conciliatory.

The collapse of the Baker-Aziz talks have left President Bush with two options: He can use force against Iraq, and in the process involve the United States in a war of uncertain duration and consequences. Or he can use the prestige of his high office to help resolve peacefully the key economic and security issues that trouble the Middle East. The President's ultimate place in history will be determined by this one decision.

The Road to the Crisis

In the months preceding Saddam's move into Kuwait, the United States was deeply involved with events in Europe. There were reports, to be sure, of Iraq's economic difficulties and of the Iraqi leader's anger at his neighbors for keeping the price of oil low. But at a moment in history when the world was celebrating the end of the old order and the radically changed superpower relationship, Iraq's economic needs were a mere footnote to history. As for the Iraqi leader, Washington knew him to be a "bully," but one who would generally fall in line with America's wishes.

The massing of Iraqi troops near Kuwait late in July was detected by U.S. intelligence satellites, but Saddam's actual plans to invade were not. When the invasion actually came to pass, on August 2, a stunned world wondered whether Saudi Arabia would be next. The United States had no treaty commitment with Kuwait and technically was under no obligation to react. Still, the invasion of a small country by its more powerful neighbor made a strong Hitler analogy. The analogy was strongest in the minds of President Bush and of former British Prime Minister Margaret Thatcher, who happened to be touring the United States at the time.

Within days of the Iraqi invasion, President Bush had committed the United States to a military solution. He ordered 200,000 troops to the Gulf--to defend Saudi Arabia, not to free Kuwait--convinced the U.N. Security Council of the need to impose and enforce sanctions, and began delivering a daily barrage of oral ultimatums to Iraq. The decisions behind all these actions were clearly the President's only. In the critical hours that national security policy was being formulated, before the actual decisions were made, the President relied exclusively on the advice of a handful of like-minded White House confidants. Key Congressional leaders, senior "statesmen," and former Presidents and/or Secretaries of State and Defense were excluded from the momentous deliberations. And it is doubtful whether President Bush or anyone in his inner circle of advisers ever asked: Is Kuwait worth all this?

By mid-October, largely due to the President's efforts, Saddam had been diplomatically isolated, a military force from twenty-five nations had been deployed to the Gulf, and the U.N. sanctions were beginning to work. But the President was restless. Sanctions alone were not driving Saddam from Kuwait; if anything the Iraqi leader was exploiting America's forbearance to strengthen the defensive posture of his forces in Kuwait. The President's decision, again reached in discussions with like-minded advisers and without outside input, was for more force.

President Bush made up his mind to double the U.S. forces in the Gulf late in October. He did not formally announce his decision, however, until after the November elections. The increase was designed to insure that the U.S. commander in the area would have an "offensive option," that is, the troops needed to drive Saddam out of Kuwait. (The original rationale for the U.S. forces, it will be recalled, was to defend Saudi Arabia, not to become involved in offensive operations.) As expected, Capitol Hill was taken aback by the sudden change in strategy. Converting Desert Shield to Desert Storm not only meant certain war, but had ominous implications for America's position in the Arab world.

By upping the ante, President Bush in effect abandoned sanctions as a means of forcing Iraq to evacuate Kuwait and gambled that Saddam would back down in view of the awesome military power confronting him. But the U.N.-imposed January 15 deadline only seems to be hardening Saddam's resolve. He is digging his heels in

Kuwait, openly reaffirming it as Iraq's 19th province, and turning his back on a number of diplomatic initiatives designed to give him a convenient exit. The President had clearly misjudged Saddam.

Diplomacy Scorned

War, if (when) it comes, will be a tragic indictment of the failure of diplomacy.

Diplomacy made it possible for the United States and the Soviet Union to reconcile many of their differences after forty-five years of cold war, enabled the Israelis and Egyptians to make peace at Camp David, made possible the reunification of Germany--but is unable to bridge the differences between President Bush and Saddam Hussein over Kuwait?

The sad truth is that diplomacy is not being given a chance to work. To be sure, there is activity out there: Diplomats are crisscrossing the continents, intermediaries are holding talks, and peace plans are proliferating. What is missing, however, is a willingness on the part of both principals to *negotiate* to give and take a little and to back off from the extreme positions that they are now publicly advocating. Listening to the rhetoric from Washington and Baghdad, it appears as if a war of unknown duration and consequences is preferable by far to a peace achieved through diplomacy, which invariably implies some form of compromise.

Our own President, for instance, is essentially offering Iraq a choice between capitulation and war. Get out of Kuwait, he warns, or else. He rejects outright the one area in which a diplomatic compromise appears promising, namely, the concurrent resolution of the Palestinian problem. Linking the two issues, he asserts, would be a concession to Saddam, even though the United States as a matter of policy has plans to address the Palestinian issue at an "appropriate future date." What in effect the President is saying is that he prefers war rather than accelerating the timing for the negotiations on the Palestinian problem.

For his part, Saddam has been more concerned since the onset of the Kuwait crisis with orchestrating an anti-American front and obtaining psychological gains from his adventure than in addressing rationally the many concerns raised by the world community because of his action. His publicity stunt of using hostages as human shields at key military installations and the daily parade through his office of a wide range of former politicians and peace activists, while refusing a visit by the U.S. Secretary of State, are clear indications of his contempt for the art of diplomacy and of its potential for resolving the issue peacefully.

When the history of the Kuwait crisis is eventually written, one aspect will stand out: diplomacy was never given a chance to settle the problem.

There Is Still Time for a Peace Plan

The diplomatic flurry that is accompanying the collapse of the Baker-Aziz talks provides ample evidence that the United States and Iraq have mismanaged the peace process.

The catastrophic consequences of a Gulf war require little elaboration. Civilian and military casualties in the thousands are all but assured, as is the devastation of the region's oil infrastructure. Millions in oil-dependent nations would suffer through higher oil prices, increased inflation, and severe economic dislocations (see Appendix B).

Such unprecedented catastrophe appears imminent, because of the unyielding refusal of the United States and of Iraq to conduct a meaningful negotiating process. Since the outset of the crisis, both nations have set such hard and uncompromising positions, have announced them publicly and staked their reputations on them, as to make a peaceful resolution of their differences impossible. The U.S. demand, for instance, that Iraq withdraw from Kuwait unconditionally ignores completely whatever merit there might be in Iraq's request that the problem of the Palestinian homeland also be considered. Iraq's rigid position similarly has precluded compromise or other diplomatic arrangement. Iraq refuses to admit that it has violated the rules of international behavior by invading Kuwait, and is unwilling to even discuss this without linkage to the Palestinian problem. Compounding the refusal of the two principals to *discuss and compromise* is the absence of the United Nations as a trustworthy intermediary and neutral third party. This is the role that the international organization has traditionally performed between feuding parties. This time, though, the United Nations finds itself as one of the warring parties unable to intercede or to use its influence toward a practical solution.

Still, it would be a tragedy and an act of international irresponsibility to abandon efforts at peacemaking. As a first step, the United States and Iraq should put an end to their rhetoric and ultimatums. Enough has already been said about "massive" and "decisive" wars, of "flattening Baghdad," and of Americans "swimming in their blood." No purpose is served by repeating these threats; the world is well aware of the positions of the two sides. It is important, too, that the Secretary General of the United Nations be allowed to reassert the international organization's role as a peacemaker--not a war party--and take time to develop a plan that addresses the legitimate grievances of both parties. A delay of thirty days for this purpose would be a sound investment, if it could avert a catastrophic war.

Concerning Iraq's conquest of Kuwait, there is consensus in the international community that the action was wrong and that it should be reversed. The most effective way to bring this about would be by means of face-to-face talks between Iraq and Kuwait to resolve the three issues outstanding between them: the timing for the withdrawal of the Iraqi forces, reparations or other restitutions due Kuwait because of the invasion of its territory, and postconflict arrangements for possible Iraqi access to Kuwait's Warba and Bubiyan Islands. Once agreement on these issues is reached, the international sanctions against Iraq can be lifted and the U.N. forces can withdraw from the Gulf.

As important as the resolution of the Kuwait issue is, a renewed international effort is required to address and resolve the underlying security issues of the region and to enhance its long-term stability. The appropriate forum for addressing these issues would be a "Middle East Security Conference" patterned after the "Conference on Confidence and Security Building Measures and Disarmament in Europe". The conference would address and hopefully resolve the two critical issues that threaten the peace and stability of the area: the increasing proliferation of nuclear, chemical, and biological weapons and the persisting territorial aggrandizement plans of certain nations in the area. The two issues are interrelated; therefore they need to be addressed together.

With U.S. leadership and goodwill on all sides, a great deal could be accomplished at such a conference. Agreements could be reached, for instance, on the inviolability of the international frontiers in the region (the 1990 German/Polish accord could serve as a guide) and for beginning the slow process of controlling the weapons of mass destruction and ultimately designating the Middle East as a "Nuclear and Chemical Weapons Free Zone." The possibilities for enhancing the security of the area through multilateral arms-control agreements would be endless.

As the January 15 deadline approaches, it is essential that the United Nations reassert its role as the international peacemaking body. The Kuwait issue is important and must be resolved. It is equally important, however, that the security concerns of the Middle East also be addressed. The alternative is a potentially long and devastating war, with thousands of civilian and military casualties and little hope for rectifying the basic ills that repeatedly plunge this area into conflict.

The Linkage Issue

The United States insists that there can be no linkage of the Gulf crisis to the broader Arab-Israeli conflict, for to do so would constitute appeasement. At an appropriate future date, asserts Secretary of State Baker, an international conference could be convened to address this issue, but not now. Are we then to understand that the United States is prepared to fight a war merely to avoid convening now an Arab-Israeli peace conference?

A quarter century after the 1967 war between Israel and its neighbors, Israel is still in control of the territorial spoils of that war-- the West Bank, the Gaza strip, Jerusalem, and the Golan Heights-- and the Palestinians are still minus a homeland. Arabs from Morocco to Bangladesh condemn the Israelis for the status quo, but also, to no lesser degree, the United States. Israel would have been obliged years ago to reach an accommodation with its Arab neighbors, they declare, had it not been for its very close relationship with the United States and the extraordinary financial and diplomatic assistance granted the Israeli state by Washington.

By its past failure to nudge Israel toward an accommodation with its Arab neighbors and its insistence that the matter be deferred once more, the United States is in effect handing Saddam Hussein an issue of enormous emotional importance among Arabs worldwide. Deep-rooted Arab memories of the extraordinary U.S. support to Israel and the double standard applied in the United Nations when dealing with the Israeli occupation of Palestinian lands as opposed to Iraq's occupation of Kuwait are making Saddam the champion of the Palestinians and America the archenemy of millions.

January 12, 1991

THE CONGRESS BACKS THE PRESIDENT

Sanctions Need Time

Much of the debate in Congress concerns the economic sanctions imposed on Iraq and whether they should be given more time to work.

Even strong supporters of the administration who favor a military solution to the Kuwait crisis admit that Iraq has suffered very substantial economic losses because of the sanctions. The international blockade has cut off 97 percent of all its exports, stopped 90 percent of its imports, and reduced its gross national product by 50 percent. Iraq's military capabilities are slowly eroding, and Saddam has not realized a single cent from his conquest of Kuwait. Still, assert the prowar advocates, sanctions are proving incapable of reversing the status quo and Iraq's annexation of Kuwait is continuing, with Saddam showing no inclination to comply with the U.N.-imposed deadline of January 15.

Sanctions on Iraq, it will be recalled, were imposed early in August 1990. They affect all aspects of that nation's economy, except for a few categories of humanitarian goods that are permitted to enter the country. Since August 25, the sanctions have been backed up by an extensive maritime interception effort involving warships from many nations.

Repeatedly, during late summer and early fall, we were assured by the Bush administration that the sanctions were "working." That view changed radically, however, soon after the 1990 congressional elections. Suddenly, the sanctions are not working; at most, we are being told, they are causing an economic hardship on a nation already accustomed to shortages and improvisations. Less than five months after their adoption, the international sanctions against Iraq have run out of time as far as the Bush administration is concerned.

It is absurd to expect any sanctions to be effective within only five months. Sanctions take time to work, and in the case of Iraq they are working now, and as time goes on, they will become even more potent. The Iraqi sanctions enjoy the unprecedented cooperation of all nations. Everything moving in and out of the country is affected, their economy is tumbling, and despite the Iraqis' admitted facility to improvise, their nation should be in desperate economic straits within another year. Sanctions may be slow, but they must be weighed against the war alternative, which is worse.

The Bush administration should give sanctions more time to work. It makes little sense to rush to war when sanctions only can accomplish the same objective. The correct policy for the United States is to continue the economic sanctions as the most cost-effective means of forcing Iraq out of Kuwait.

Random Thoughts During the Congressional Debate

During much of January 11 and 12, 1991, the Congress has been debating the use of force in the Gulf (see Appendix C). It is a magnificent demonstration of our democratic freedoms, but also of the awesome political power that we have allowed our presidents to accumulate. At the end, the President has skillfully worked Congress into his corner. The final vote in the Senate is 52 to 47 for the use of military force; in the House of Representatives, 250 to 183.

Can President Bush convince the nation that war over Kuwait is worth the price? He has been successful in marshalling a worldwide coalition against Saddam, but can he also unite America?

Many members of Congress are saying that they are supporting the President because a vote authorizing the use of force will enhance the prospects of peace. Now that is twisted logic! How can peace be realized by going to war?

The President appears to be in such a great hurry to embrace the war option. Has he exhausted all other alternatives?

Why are the risks and costs of this venture being borne so overwhelmingly by the United States? There are over 400,000 U.S. troops in the Gulf, but fewer than 50,000 Europeans. Yet Europe gets most its oil from this region. And what about Japan and Germany? Have we become their mercenaries?

It is obvious that all members of the Senate and the House support the President's initial decision to deploy forces in Saudi Arabia, as well as his actions relating to the embargo. But the President's decision of last November, which increased the number of troops in the Persian Gulf to 430,000 to attain a "credible offensive" option, was taken without consultation with them. Why was there no public debate over that issue, ask the President's critics?

War in the Gulf, claims one of the speakers, would carry enormous risks, an unknown number of casualties, billions of dollars spent, a greatly disrupted oil supply, possible involvement of Israel, Turkey, and other allies, the possible long-term occupation of Iraq, increased instability in the Gulf region, and long-lasting Arab enmity against the United States.

A great many legislators appear to be supporting the President because of fear that the U.N. coalition will not last much longer, that the sanctions will disintegrate. Is this sufficient reason to go to war?

Iraq has not attacked us; it has not claimed a single American life; why should we be concerned?

January 15, 1991

WHEN THE WAR COMES

At the United Nations, the Security Council is debating a French plan. Reportedly, the United States is opposed to it. Today Iraq must evacuate Kuwait or face war. Will fighting actually start tomorrow?

The Uncertainties of War

As the U.N.-imposed deadline is approaching, the stalemate in the Gulf continues. Iraq is still in control of Kuwait, the United States continues to insist on an unconditional withdrawal, and efforts at resolving the crisis peacefully are going nowhere. War is all but certain.

War, of course, is always unpredictable, and a great deal can go wrong once the shooting starts. In the case of the military action contemplated in the Gulf, five major uncertainties are especially troubling: (1) How long will the war last? (2) Who will be fighting on our side? (3) Will Israel become involved? (4) How will the Soviet Union react? (5) Will Iraq use weapons of mass destruction?

With regard to the first uncertainty, as the party initiating military action, we have the upper hand in deciding what kind a war this will be, whether an air only or an air-land-sea war. (The official line is that the U.S. assault will come "suddenly" and will be "massive and decisive.") We cannot predict, however, how strong an opposition the Iraqis will put up. It is folly to assume that we can "finish off" Saddam in a few days or within a couple of weeks, when in fact it is impossible to estimate the duration of the conflict with any degree of accuracy. Our troops may require a few days, a couple of weeks, or perhaps much, much longer. Also, once the fighting starts it will be very difficult to limit the contest to the geographic area of Kuwait only. Our own inclination will be to drive into Baghdad and remove Saddam from the scene forever. For his part, the Iraqi leader will undoubtedly attempt to broaden the war into a regionwide confrontation of Arabs versus Americans. There is simply no way of predicting how the war will evolve or how long it will last. Vietnam and Afghanistan should serve as examples.

Related are uncertainties over our "allies." About twenty nations have dispatched forces (some sizable, but mostly very small) to the Gulf, but whether these forces will actually fight alongside U.S. forces is totally speculative. Only Great Britain thus far has promised to help. The remaining nations, including Turkey, a NATO ally that borders Iraq, are sitting on the fence.

The critical allies, of course, would be the Arab members of the U.N. coalition, primarily Kuwait, Saudi Arabia, Egypt, and Syria. Kuwait has no military forces of any consequence, so its contribution would be minimal. Saudi Arabia's contribution could be substantial but is uncertain. The Saudis would put up a stiff fight to defend their nation, but joining the United States in a war to liberate Kuwait is a totally different matter. Their attitude all along has been that they have invited the U.S. forces on their territory for "defensive" purposes, that is, to protect the kingdom from Saddam. Nothing has been said, officially at least, of a Saudi participation in a Kuwait war. Chances are even smaller that the Egyptian and Syrian U.N. coalition forces will end up fighting alongside the Americans, especially if Israel becomes involved in the war.

From the outset of the crisis, Israel, at considerable risk to its own security, has behaved with utmost composure. At U.S. urging and in exchange of a U.S. pledge not to link the Kuwait issue with that of a Palestinian settlement, Israel has kept a low profile and has avoided actions likely to provoke the Iraqi leader. But all bets will be off should the Israelis detect unmistaken evidence of Iraqi preparations to strike their territory. The Israeli preemptive and/or retaliatory strikes will play havoc with the U.S. strategy of maintaining an Arab consensus against Iraq. It is inconceivable for any Arab nation to fight alongside the Israelis against another Arab nation.

The Soviet Union's reaction to a Gulf war represents yet another major uncertainty. Over the past months, Moscow has generally acquiesced to U.S. efforts in dealing with the Iraqi aggression, in the process even placing at risk its long-standing military and economic relationship with Iraq. But Soviet policies appear to be changing, with the departure of Soviet Foreign Minister Edward Shevardnadze and the ascendancy in the Kremlin of conservative Communist party leaders. The question logically arises: When the United States decides to strike, will Moscow look the other way as it did in Panama, or is it likely to resume its former pro-Arab stance?

The probability that Iraq will use weapons of mass destruction similarly represents a major uncertainty. Its arsenal of chemical and bacteriological weapons (backed by missiles capable of reaching U.S. troop assembly areas and depots) is considered threatening enough to have required the issuance of specialized protective gear and of other countermeasures. Major U.S. losses could result from a sudden and massive chemical and/or bacteriological attack.

Iraq clearly understands the above enormous uncertainties confronting the United States. Its defiance of U.N. resolutions and stubborn determination to hang on to the conquered lands reflects judgment in Baghdad that the United States would be foolhardy to attempt a military solution in light of these uncertainties.

For its part, Iraq too is confronted with uncertainties, making the outcome of a military confrontation with the United States equally unpredictable. The issues that trouble the United States (the likely duration of the war, the loyalty of allies, Israel's possible involvement, the Soviet Union's ultimate posture, and the possibility that weapons of mass destruction may be used) are as applicable to Baghdad as they are to Washington. Iraq's uncertainties are additionally compounded by geography. The nation shares borders with five nations--Iran, Turkey, Syria, Jordan, and Saudi Arabia--all of which would not hesitate to snatch portions of the Iraqi carcass after the United States is finished with it.

Concerning the possibility of U.S. use of chemical and/or nuclear weapons, Iraq can never be sure. As a signatory to the Geneva Protocol, the United States is precluded from using chemical weapons, although it obviously has the capability for doing so. A similar legal prohibition does not exist for nuclear weapons, but it is inconceivable that the United States would cross the nuclear threshold as part of a Kuwait war. Still, as Baghdad has undoubtedly noted, the U.S. naval forces in the Gulf have extensive nuclear capabilities.

With such major uncertainties confronting both sides--not considering the military and civilian casualties likely to result from the war and the anticipated certain devastation of the oil infrastructure in the entire Gulf region--does a war over Kuwait make sense? Is not a peace settlement, even though imperfect, in the interest of both parties? The obvious answer is yes. A peace settlement now with no victors or losers would be far more preferable to one dictated later, after great pain and suffering, by the victor of the engagement. The fact is so obvious that one wonders why Washington and Baghdad are having such great difficulty recognizing it.

The U.N. Coalition

As war is approaching, we are being reminded regularly that twenty-eight nations have deployed forces in the Gulf. Presumably this supports the case for war. Still, it requires no special military expertise to realize that only four of the nations in the coalition-- Great Britain, France, Saudi Arabia, and Egypt--have deployed forces in the Gulf that are militarily substantial. All other forces arrayed against Saddam are either very small, have limited missions, or were sent to the area for symbolic value. The forces that should have been there, those of the industrialized nations of Europe and Asia that depend heavily on Middle East oil (Germany, Japan, China, and Korea, to name a few) are not. Neither are those of the other superpower.

How many of the nations in the U.N. coalition will actually fight when the order is given is a major uncertainty. The Secretary of State asserts that all will, except possibly for Syria and for some small nations whose parliaments must first give approval to such action. The United States is pressuring Turkey to join the fight, too, but this "staunch" U.S. ally appears to be more interested in obtaining increased U.S. military aid and financial assistance than in shedding blood over Kuwait. As for Israel, it has sent no forces to the Gulf and continues to maintain a low profile at the request of the United States, but has officially announced that it reserves the right to defend itself should it be attacked.

The key ally, of course, is Saudi Arabia. From the outset of the crisis, the Saudis have maintained that the purpose of the military forces stationed on their territory was to defend the kingdom. Reportedly the Saudi policy is changing and King Fahd is now prepared to join the United States in an offensive war against Iraq.

The prospect of Arabs fighting alongside Americans against other Arabs has most Middle East experts wondering how long this arrangement will last. More important, will the U.S.-Arab coalition hold should Israel become involved in the war?

Casualties: Theirs and Ours

The last time American forces were ordered into battle, during operation Just Cause in Panama, twenty-six GIs and at least six hundred civilians lost their lives. The operation lasted a few hours and involved a tiny fraction of the forces now poised to strike Iraq. Should we go to war over Kuwait, what would be our casualties?

What about Iraq's military losses and the casualties among the civilian populations of the Gulf area? The stated U.S. intention is to avoid another Vietnam and to strike "suddenly, massively, and decisively." It all sounds so ominous! Vietnam, it will be recalled, was a "low-intensity" conflict fought over "limited" objectives. Still it cost us about 58,000 dead.

Most Washington war gurus are busy these days predicting the type and length of the war and what casualties we are likely to take. Congressman Les Aspin (D-Wis.), for instance, Chairman of the House Armed Services Committee, is predicting a war of massive air strikes, escalating a week or so later into a ground battle to recapture Kuwait. Should Iraq collapse early, he asserts, American casualties would be "moderate," about 3,000 to 5,000, including up to 1,000 deaths. A more protracted war could result in casualties of up to 20,000, including more than 3,000 deaths. The Pentagon, of course, is silent on the matter. But it does note that Iraq has moved into the Kuwait theater of operations more than 540,000 troops, supported by approximately 4,000 tanks, 3,000 artillery pieces, and 500 combat aircraft.

In view of the many uncertainties--political as well as military--that this war will entail, how can anyone honestly attempt a prediction of casualties? We will be entering the conflict as a member of an alliance of NATO and Arab nations that is extremely frail and that could come apart the very moment Israel becomes militarily involved. Much of our key equipment, especially that planned for use in the air campaign against Iraq, has never before seen combat. Its performance is uncertain. Weather conditions, too, could adversely affect ground and air operations at critical junctures of the war. The enemy, battle-tested and seasoned, could profit from any combination of mistakes on our part and good luck on his. There is simply no way for anyone to predict how long this war will last or how many men and women we and the other side will lose.

As for civilian casualties, no war has ever been fought when civilians did not suffer. It is the nature of combat to involve innocent civilians and to waste them, at times, in much higher numbers than the losses sustained by the forces actually doing the fighting. Especially during the twentieth century, civilian populations have become fair game to a multitude of weapons: cannon shells, mortars, air-delivered bombs, missiles, chemical and even nuclear weapons.

Again no reliable prediction is possible of anticipated civilian losses. Most civilian casualties will undoubtedly occur during the air phase of the conflict, either because of air strikes designed to terrorize local populations (such as the threatened missile strikes on Israeli cities by Iraq) or because of pilot error. During the ground war, the types of weapons used, the intensity of fire, and the discipline of troops will be significant factors determining the level of losses sustained by the civilians in the combat area.

Short of an enormous provocation on the part of Iraq, it is highly unlikely that the United States will use weapons of mass destruction in its war of liberation of Kuwait. Under the Geneva Protocol of 1925, the United States is committed against the use of chemical weapons, and it is all but certain that it will observe that prohibition. As for nuclear weapons, their use against Iraq is totally improbable. Their use would create more problems than it would alleviate. Then, too, the United States has in the past promised to refrain from using nuclear weapons against any nonnuclear weapons state that has acceded to the Non-Proliferation Treaty. Iraq is one such state.

War Objectives and Outcome Scenarios

Attempting to predict how the war will evolve brings to mind World War II. Who could have predicted in August 1939 that the war would last five and a half years, that sixty nations would eventually become involved, and that as a result of the war, the empires of the era would collapse, the United States and the Soviet Union would achieve superpower status, and Japan and Germany would become the economic giants they are today? Predicting what will happen in the Gulf and how the fighting will end clearly falls in the realm of impossible.

Although it has never formally said so, the United States appears to have four military objectives as it enters the war: (1) to liberate Kuwait and return the Emir to power; (2) to drastically reduce Iraq's military capabilities so that they no longer are a menace to Israel and to the other nations in the region; (3) to destroy Iraq's chemical and nuclear weapons facilities; and (4) to remove from power Saddam Hussein and his immediate circle of lieutenants. In the view of members of the Bush administration, achievement of these objectives is an essential precondition for a U.S. leadership role in the Gulf and for introducing peace and stability into the region.

Patriotism and bravado aside, achievement by the U.S. military of all four stated objectives is by no means assured. There are at least three war outcome scenarios possible, each resulting in a radically altered Gulf region and U.S. role.

The least likely of all possible postwar scenarios--one, that hopefully will never materialize--would result from a U.S. military defeat at the hands of Iraq. Under this scenario the U.S. war effort would turn sour by a combination of inconclusive air strikes, a protracted stalemate on the ground, collapse of the U.N. coalition, and massive opposition to the war at home. The United States, unable to achieve any of its stated objectives, except possibly the destruction of Iraq's chemical and nuclear production capability, would decide to call it quits. Left behind to chart their own dubious future would be America's Arab allies, a victorious Saddam, and a threatened Israel. Anti-Americanism would abound throughout the region, and America's hopes for guiding the Gulf into a new era of peace and stability would have been shattered.

In contrast, the United States would be kneedeep in Gulf problems under either of the two postwar scenarios that are likely to prevail. The first--the "cease-fire" scenario--would result from a protracted war at which neither side could gain the upper hand. A cease-fire negotiated by Arab intermediaries would end the shooting but solve none of the region's basic ills, except possibly for the withdrawal of Iraq from Kuwait and the restoration of the Emir to his throne. Two important U.S. military objectives would remain unfulfilled: Iraq would still be a substantial military power able to threaten its neighbors, and Saddam Hussein would continue to be the Iraqi leader. The "cease-fire" scenario would confront the United States with all of the region's prewar problems--Hussein and his war machine, endemic instability, weapons of mass destruction, an environment of intimidation and insecurity--and would frustrate hopes for the introduction of a "new order." The Arab-Israeli conflict, proliferation of nuclear and chemical weapons, and oil rivalries would continue to plague the region. Under the parameters of this scenario, the war with Iraq would have accomplished nothing, except possibly to inflame Arab anti-Americanism and to increase the region's instability. History would merely record it as another sad chapter of

Middle East warfare, alongside the four Arab-Israeli wars, the eight-year Iran-Iraq war, and Lebanon's fifteen-year-old civil strife.

A far more complex situation would confront the United States as a result of a war-end scenario that presupposes a swift and complete U.S. victory over Iraq and the achievement by the United States of all four of its military objectives. Saddam would be either dead or in jail and Iraq in ruins, with major parts of its territory under the control of opportunistic neighbors. A Pax Americana would ensue, with the United States assuming the role of the final arbiter, prescribing solutions to the Arab-Israeli conflict, to oil disputes, and to issues of weapons proliferation. Large contingents of U.S. air, ground, and naval forces would be forced to remain in the area to serve as "peace keepers," but actually to provide a "fire brigade" for putting out fires and conflicts in the region. The United States would be more deeply involved in the Middle East than it ever was in Europe during the days of the Cold War.

Ignoring for an instant the consequences of the first of the above scenarios, and assuming that either the cease-fire or the Pax Americana version prevails, is this what America wants? Is it prepared for the enormous sacrifices that they both entail? All this because of Kuwait?

Have All Wars Been As Unpredictable?

How long will this one last?
How many will die?
Will the U.N. coalition hold?
What if Israel becomes involved?
How would a U.S. military victory play in the Arab world?
What if the United States prevails but there is no peace?
Who will fill the vacuum if Iraq collapses?
What will the Middle East look like after the war?
Is Kuwait worth it all?

January 16, 1991

January 15 has come and gone and Saddam is still in Kuwait. The President has informed Congress (see Appendix D) that U.S.

diplomatic efforts to obtain Iraqi compliance with the appropriate U.N. resolutions has failed. At the United Nations the French peace initiative has collapsed. It would have linked Iraq's evacuation of Kuwait to an international conference to address the Palestinian problem, a position opposed by the United States. It is no longer *whether*, but *when* the war will start.

Why Should War Be The Only Option?

Why is the United States blocking all last-minute attempts at a peaceful settlement? Why is any solution, short of Iraq's total capitulation, unacceptable to Washington?

Of course, Saddam has violated the norms of international behavior by his invasion of Kuwait. But why the sudden insistence on the need to uphold international law, when similar cases of aggression in the past have gone unnoticed? Were not Afghanistan, East Timor, Chad, Cyprus, Lebanon, the West Bank and Gaza, Western Sahara similarly violated by their more powerful neighbors while the world looked the other way?

2 The Air Battle

January 17, 1991

LAUNCHING OPERATION DESERT STORM

The long-threatened war to force the Iraqis out of Kuwait started at about 2:30 a.m. on January 17, 1991, when U.S. and allied forces struck military targets in Baghdad and elsewhere in Iraq and Kuwait. In a televised address to the nation, President Bush announced that the liberation of Kuwait had begun. The code name for the operation is Desert Storm.

The Weapons of War

The war to liberate Kuwait is hardly a few hours old and already we are learning to recognize its sounds and symbols. "Surgical air strikes," "smart bombs," "stealth bombers," "cruise missiles," terms strange and confusing until yesterday, are suddenly coming to life under a deluge of reports and analyses provided by official Washington and dozens of self-anointed military experts. An identical theme pervades all reports: the President has ordered into the Gulf the best, most modern, most sophisticated weapons in the U.S. arsenal; nothing is being held back. Our air weapons, originally designed to penetrate the highly forbidding Soviet space, should have no difficulty smashing Iraq's frail air defense environment.

Let's hope so--but, also, how sad!

Unusual emotions of pride and patriotism, but also of sadness, greet the early news from the front. U.S. and allied forces are enjoying enormous success over the skies of Iraq, dropping bombs at will, destroying key Iraqi targets, literally pulverizing Saddam's chemical and nuclear weapons potential. But there are also losses: in planes lost, in pilots killed or captured, in innocent civilians maimed, in America's standing in the world and among our own children, and in our economy, which suddenly feels threatened and uncertain.

Three weapons are competing for most of the headlines: the Tomahawk cruise missile, the Patriot antimissile missile, and the F-117A "stealth" attack fighter. All untested and unproven until now, they are performing magnificently under wartime conditions. They are only the tip of the iceberg. America's argument with Saddam is being settled by an enormous fleet of U.S. aircraft: B-52G and F-111 long-range bombers, AWACS warning planes, F-16s, F-15s, F/A 18s, and much, much more. They are all part of the "tool box"--a new Pentagon term--available to General Norman Schwarzkopf, the commander in the area, to do his job.

What a waste! One cannot help but wonder what the cost of this incessant U.S. bombing must be. Thousands of individual pieces of ordnance are being expended plus the wear and tear and losses of the aircraft delivering them. Each Tomahawk, for instance, of which we have probably fired several hundred, reportedly costs $1.3 million; each Patriot $1.1 million. For the cost of the Tomahawk and Patriots alone, fired during the first few hours of the war, we could have educated hundreds of young Americans to be engineers and scientists.

Yes, there is pride in the news from the front. There is pride in America's science and technology that has helped design and build the weapons enjoying such great success, and for the thousands of young men and women who are so adept at using them. Who can gaze, for instance, at the sleek, new F-117A and not sense enormous pride? The plane's unique shape, materials, and engineering have allowed it to enter and exit the skies of Iraq practically undetected. And what about all those electronic gadgets and black boxes on our aircraft that have made Iraq's air defenses irrelevant?

Nothing tells the story of the past few days better than the total absence from the skies of Saddam's air force. Iraq's planes are nowhere to be seen, despite the droves of U.S. and allied aircraft roaming overhead. Yet Iraq, according to the Pentagon, owns at least seven hundred first-rate planes, including Soviet-built MIG-29 fighters and SU-24 bombers, and the French-built F-1 Mirage fighter. The only Iraqi weapon that has made an appearance thus far has been the pathetic Scud, a weapon of no military significance except perhaps as a means of terror. Scuds are one of the Soviet Union's many legacies to Iraq. Built by Soviet engineers and sold to the Iraqis as a weapon capable of reaching targets beyond the range of artillery, Scuds are notoriously slow, inaccurate, and operationally insignificant.

Terror over Tel Aviv and Haifa

Saddam had repeatedly threatened to strike Israel with surface-to-surface missiles at the very instant U.S. forces attacked his country. On the morning hours of January 18 he made good on his threat. Scud missiles landed on Tel Aviv and Haifa, sending the panicky residents of the two Israeli coastal cities scrambling to their shelters to don their gas masks (the intruding missiles fortunately carried no chemical weapons).

The missile attack and similar attacks that followed represent a futile effort by the Iraqi leader to draw the Jewish state into the Gulf war and in the process cause a major breach in the allied coalition. Three factors are foiling his plan: the futility of the Scuds as weapons of war and their inability to cause any significant damage to Israeli military targets, the surprisingly high effectiveness of the U.S. Patriot antimissile missiles in defending against the Scuds, and the strength of the U.S.-Israeli relationship, which is inducing Israel to hold its fire in the interest of the U.S.-led coalition.

That the Scuds would prove ineffectual as weapons of war was never in doubt. Saddam had used them before, during his eight-year war against Iran, so their limitations had been thoroughly documented by U.S. military analysts and certainly also by the Israelis. Scuds come in three versions: the basic configuration, which has a range of about 175 miles, and two Iraqi-modified versions (the Al-Hussein and the Al-Abbas), with about twice that range. Modifying the Scuds to give them more range has decreased their accuracy and also the weight of the ordnance they can carry. Over Iran and on their attacks against Israeli cities, Scuds have at times drifted as much as 3,000 yards from their intended targets.

The persisting Iraqi Scud attacks against Israel are not only raising the odds that Israel will ultimately retaliate, they are also placing the United States in a grave quandary. Israel wants assurances that the remaining Scuds will be taken out promptly--assurances that the United States is unable to give. (U.S. military intelligence simply does not know how many Scuds Iraq had at the beginning of the war or how many it might still have.) Without such assurances, Israel is threatening to retaliate. In the meantime, the United States is combing the Iraqi countryside for evidence of Scuds and is rushing additional Patriot batteries to Israel to help protect its civilian population.

Two critical questions linger: Will the U.S. efforts designed to keep Israel out of the Gulf war succeed? If Israel does lose its cool and decides to retaliate, how will the Arab members of the U.N. coalition react to the sight of Jews killing their Arab brothers?

Is the War Going Well?

U.S. and allied air forces have been raiding Iraq and Kuwait for several days now, using the very best in aircraft and enjoying almost total freedom on the skies. Still, no one in authority in Washington or Riyadh wants to venture a judgment on the results of the battle.

This is not Vietnam, we are being reminded. In Vietnam it was easy. A company commander returning to Saigon after a search and destroy mission knew precisely how many guerrillas he had killed and how many others had escaped. But this is not the case with a pilot returning from a mission in Baghdad. All the instant communications and precision-guided arms notwithstanding, there is no way for the command in Riyadh to know how well a particular bombing raid went.

In the high-tech war to force Iraq out of Kuwait, evaluating the effectiveness of the air campaign is the role of "bomb damage assessment," or BDA, as our military prefer to call it. The trouble with BDA, explains the Pentagon apologetically, is that it is slow and imprecise and is made more difficult by bad weather and a cunning enemy, which the Iraqis presumably are. BDA relies on the memory of pilots, which is not always very good, and on photographs, which, although great in terms of technical quality, must first be "interpreted" by people. Since aircraft crews seldom linger long enough over a target to make a visual observation of the results of their raid and photography is often hindered by bad weather, reconciling bomb damage information from photography and claims made by pilots can at times be frustrating.

Judgment on the success or failure of the air campaign is also hampered, according to military briefers in Riyadh and Washington, by Iraqi actions. The Iraqis are extremely resourceful at adapting to the battle environment and have displayed skill at building decoys and camouflaging sites. Repeatedly, since the beginning of the air war, they have repaired damage caused by U.S. planes, but without making these repairs visible from the air, so as not to lure the American bombers back again to the same targets. By deploying decoys and making emergency repairs, the Iraqis are reportedly attempting to blunt the worst effects of the U.S. bombing.

BDA is also experiencing serious problems in its attempts to evaluate the combat effectiveness of the Iraqi troops hidden in bunkers in Kuwait. A very dense network of decoys exists in the area, making it extremely difficult to discriminate between real tanks and artillery, and decoys. The search through the Iraqi countryside for evidence of additional mobile Scud missiles is similarly frustrating. (It's like trying to "find a needle in a haystack," complained General Schwarzkopf recently.) The Iraqi missiles are small and compact and can be fired from just about any location. Baghdad still has hundreds of Scuds hidden in warehouses, beneath bridges or even in tunnels, making it very difficult for U.S. spy satellites to recognize them or to set them apart from other similar-looking objects.

How is the air campaign going thus far? Five days into the war, only BDA knows for sure. The Pentagon is not saying and neither is the command in Riyadh.

Operation Desert Storm Is on Schedule

On January 23, 1991, President Bush described Operation Desert Storm as being right on schedule. But the war, he warned, will be neither short nor easy. General Colin Powell, Chairman of the Joint Chiefs of Staff, echoed the same sentiments when he noted, "Our strategy to go after the Iraqi army is very, very simple.

First we're going to cut it off, and then we're going to kill it.
We are in no hurry."

Air Superiority and Air Supremacy

A curious debate has been ongoing in Washington and Riyadh
during the past three days concerning the effectiveness of the air war.
It centers on the question whether the U.S. and allied air forces have
attained "supremacy" over the skies of Iraq or a mere "superiority."
Does it really matter? By all accounts, U.S. and allied aircraft are
raining destruction over Iraq, taking out targets at will with pinpoint
accuracy and devastating Iraqi lines of communication and supply
routes to the dug-in troops in Kuwait. The level of devastation is such
that the U.S. forces may even be spared the need to go after
Saddam's troops on the ground.
The debate on "superiority" versus "supremacy" is outright
ludicrous. The occasional firing of Scuds notwithstanding, the U.S.
and coalition air forces are in total control of the Iraqi airspace and
victory seems all but assured.

Keeping Civilian Casualties Down

Adding to the euphoria of good news from the front is the fact that
casualties to date among the civilian populations of Iraq and Kuwait
have been extremely low. Despite the thousands of tons of explosives
we and the allied air forces have delivered since the beginning of the
war, only a few civilians reportedly have lost their lives. That is good
news!
It is of course nearly impossible to know for sure. Our military says
it does not have exact numbers. The few Western reporters still in
Iraq probably know but are not allowed to say (their reports are
heavily censored by Iraqi authorities), and Iraq's claims are just that,
"claims" designed to inflame the Arab world against the United States.
Refugees from Iraq report having heard rumors of dead civilians, but
they, too, confirm that the number of war victims is probably
relatively small.
Reports on civilian casualties that originate in Iraq are heavily

slanted to portray intentional U.S. targeting of civilian areas. The reports are distributed by the Iraqi Ministry of Information--Saddam's official propaganda agency--and as such are of very low credibility. Increasingly this ministry is reporting losses among civilians, as well as damage to cultural and religious shrines, hospitals, and museums. The Iraqi reports are contradicted by the United States. Air raids, asserts the Pentagon, are being aimed exclusively at military targets and every effort is being made to minimize civilian casualties (although a few Tomahawk cruise missiles may have misfired.)

The fact that Iraqi civilians have perished as a result of the U.S. and allied air raids cannot be disputed, but their numbers appear to be extremely low given the massive quantities of munitions used. This is good news--news worth cheering about!

The Cradle of Civilization

Military briefers in Washington and Riyadh have recently taken to characterizing Iraq as a "target-rich environment." The designation presumably helps to rationalize why 2,500 or so bombing sorties a day are still required against a nation of 17 million that is the size of California.

Iraq may be rich in military targets, but it is rich, too, in archaeological remains, museums, monuments, and classical sites. This is, after all, the cradle of civilization, the area where humanity's first civilization flourished 6,000 years ago, and where today some of the world's oldest and most renowned archaeological finds are located.[1]

How well are these treasures faring under the incessant U.S. and allied bombing, especially those in the vicinity of legitimate military targets? Iraq charges that some sites, including the National Museum in Baghdad, have sustained "large-scale" damage. Many Americans dismiss these charges as fabrications by Saddam designed to whip up anti-Americanism. It would be a sad commentary on the twentieth century if the priceless treasures of the cradle of civilization end up becoming victims of our thirst for oil.

Women in Combat

By law, American women are prohibited from taking part in combat. Battleships, attack aircraft, missile batteries, and tanks are all off limits to them. Their role is to "support" the men who are and will be doing the fighting, not to actually fight. About 27,000 women are seeing service in the Gulf under these rules, servicing tanks, standing guard duty outside depots, helping deliver ordnance to air crews, flying helicopters, and so on.

The official restrictions notwithstanding, American women are being drawn closer to combat duty with each passing day. With Scud and Patriot missiles soaring overhead, and the planned land battle expected to involve far-reaching maneuvers, the old limits are becoming less and less relevant. In the war zone, American women would run the same risks as men would and could end up being taken prisoner and/or getting killed. How will the folks back home react at the sight of service women returning in body bags? Or at the news that American service women, taken prisoner, are being sexually abused by Iraqi guards?

Is All Fair in War?

News from the Gulf confirm that Saddam Hussein is brutalizing American and allied prisoners, using them as human shields and otherwise violating the Geneva Conventions for the treatment of prisoners of war. He is also systematically devastating Kuwait, destroying its oil infrastructure, and threatening the ecology of the entire Persian Gulf region.

Few of Saddam's stunts have infuriated the world more than his parading on television of the brutalized faces of U.S. and allied prisoners, many making statements forced upon them by their captors. This indignity was compounded by an official announcement that the prisoners would be dispersed to selected military targets throughout Iraq, presumably to deter future allied air strikes against these targets. The entire episode is reminiscent of Saddam's treatment of thousands of foreign workers who happened to find themselves in Kuwait at the time of the Iraqi invasion. For months, these innocent victims of war were denied permission to return to their homes, being used instead as human shields at Iraqi military bases, industrial plants, and strategic sites.

Reflecting his apparent belief that all is fair in war, Saddam has also launched a massive assault on Kuwait's oil infrastructure, setting many of its oil fields on fire, destroying pipelines and terminals, and dumping millions of barrels of Kuwaiti oil into the Persian Gulf. The resulting spill, already larger than that caused by the 1989 *Exxon Valdez* mishap off the coast of Alaska, is assuming the dimensions of a major environmental catastrophe. As the oil slick is moving south, it is fouling the water, devastating the gulf's fishing industry and marine wildlife, and threatening the water desalination plant that provides much of the drinking water for Riyadh and eastern Saudi Arabia.

Saddam apologists, in Jordan and elsewhere in the Arab world, suggest that the Iraqi leader unleashed these actions because of military considerations. The oil spill at the beaches in Kuwait, they assert, will help divert a planned Marine landing against this area and prevent the loss of life among the dug-in Iraqis. As for the smoke from the burning oil wells, its purpose is to restrict the visibility of American pilots and reduce the effectiveness of their bombing raids against targets in Kuwait.

Granted that some military benefits will accrue to Saddam from his oil-related actions, do these benefits really justify the ecological carnage that he has triggered? A similar question troubles critics of the recent authorization to the U.S. commander in the Gulf that he may, under certain circumstances, use "nonlethal riot-control gasses" against the Iraqi forces.[2] With most nations of the world considering tear gas to be a chemical weapon outlawed by the Geneva Convention of 1925, does it make sense for the United States to be first in using it? Would not our use of such gas give Saddam Hussein the excuse to retaliate with mustard or nerve gas?

All is *not* fair in war. The rule applies equally to Saddam and to us.

January 29, 1991

CONTINUING UNCERTAINTIES

What Is Saddam Up To?

Three weeks into the air war, with his key command and control facilities in ruins, his air defenses maimed, and his capability for developing and producing nuclear and chemical weapons totally demolished, Saddam Hussein gives not the tiniest indication that he is prepared to enter the war. He just stands there, stoically (foolishly?) accepting blow after blow and simply refusing to fight back. Why isn't Saddam striking back? It couldn't be for want of military forces; much of his military might, especially his army and air forces, are still unused. Why, then, is he taking this awful punishment with no apparent desire to defend himself?

Persons who claim to understand Saddam's mindset assert that the Iraqi leader is fully aware that he cannot possibly win a military confrontation with the United States. His only hope, therefore, lies in a "political victory," one achieved either through the breakup of the U.N. coalition or by an early U.S. abandonment of the conflict. Saddam considers almost any war-ending scenario, short of an unconditional Iraqi surrender, to constitute a political victory, well worth the punishment he is receiving at the hands of the U.S. and coalition forces.

In view of the many military setbacks that he has experienced thus far and the enormous U.N. forces confronting him, is it not foolhardy for the Iraqi leader to expect "victory"? The answer is so obvious it hardly needs to be stated. Yet, Saddam continues to remain impervious to the destruction surrounding him, stubbornly adhering to his basic strategy of not fighting back, firing an occasional Scud at Tel Aviv or Riyadh, and preparing for what he hopes will be a protracted and grinding war of attrition with the U.S. forces on the ground.

The Scud attacks, of course, are militarily insignificant. Their purpose is to draw Israel into the war and in the process to confront America's Arab allies, especially Egypt and Syria, with an untenable political dilemma, either to fight alongside the Israelis or to pull out of the coalition, or even to switch sides. As for luring the United

States and its allies into a protracted ground war, the second element in the Saddam strategy, the casualties of a protracted ground war, Saddam hopes, will unite his own people and cause them to feel revulsion toward the West. U.S. casualties, on the other hand, will turn public opinion against the war, undermine the national resolve, and result in America's abandoning the war effort.

Israel's reluctance to enter the war and the refusal of the United States as yet to engage Iraq on the ground seem to have shattered whatever prospects for success there may be in Saddam's strategy. A major uncertainty still remains. In view of his deteriorating military condition, will the Iraqi leader persist with his no-win strategy, or is he likely to engage in doomsday options, including the use of chemical and bacteriological weapons?

The Mystery of the Escaping Iraqi Aircraft

Among the many uncertainties of this war is the mystery of the escaping Iraqi aircraft. Over one hundred and fifty of them, the best and most modern warplanes in Saddam's inventory, have taken refuge in the airfields of his former enemy, Iran. Equally surprising is Iran's reaction to the episode, allowing the incoming aircraft to land unimpeded, without even once attempting to challenge or limit their arrival.

Have Iraq and Iran, enemies until 1988, struck a secret deal that allows Saddam to save his air force from certain annihilation in the hands of the United States? Worse yet, has Iran possibly agreed to allow these planes to rejoin the war later at a place and time of Iraq's choosing? Maintaining the Iraqi aircraft and refueling them for their return flight home would clearly make Iran a combatant on the side of Saddam.

The government in Teheran claims to be neutral in the conflict and has informed the United States through intermediaries that it intends to keep the Iraqi aircraft grounded until the end of the war. It disclaims any advance knowledge or approval of the Iraqi action. Still, the welcome extended the escaping planes raises some urgent questions: What are Iran's true expectations from the war? Why would it want to offer Iraq, its bitter enemy until yesterday, a helping hand? The Iranian government has condemned Iraq's invasion of

Kuwait and has promised to honor the economic sanctions voted by the United Nations. But Iran has also condemned bitterly the U.S. buildup in the Gulf and the presence of "colonialists" near the Muslim holy sites of Jedha and Medina.

Few knowledgeable persons in Washington believe that Iran is accepting the Iraqi aircraft as a "gesture of Muslim solidarity." Iran has no warm feelings for either Iraq or America. By accepting the Iraqi aircraft for safekeeping, while also promising to keep them grounded for the duration of the war, Iran is playing both sides of the conflict against each other and for its own advantage. The sudden war in the Persian Gulf between Iran's two archenemies is a welcome development, and Teheran realizes that it has nothing to gain by getting drawn into the conflict. By playing a balancing act between the two combatants and throwing an occasional bone at the Iraqis and at the Americans, Iran is positioning itself to be a major power broker of the postwar period and a force in the region to be reckoned with.

The Chemical Threat

Three weeks into the war and Saddam Hussein has not made good on the most dreadful of all his threats: to use chemical weapons against the military and civilian populations of his enemies. The hush is unnerving. What gives? Is the Iraqi leader suddenly relenting? Saddam has never before balked at the use of chemical weapons against his enemies. He is even known to have used them against his own people.

That Saddam Hussein still holds, despite incessant U.S. and allied air raids, an enormous arsenal of chemical weapons can hardly be disputed. The raids may have devastated Iraq's capability for producing chemical weapons, but not its existing stockpiles of chemical weapons munitions. Thousands of chemical artillery shells, bombs, and missile warheads remain intact in secret underground Iraqi bunkers. This fact notwithstanding, Saddam's dread chemical artillery shells--the GI's worst nightmare--have yet to be used, and conventionally armed (rather than chemically armed) Scuds continue to strike Israel and Saudi Arabia. It all seems odd, especially in light of Saddam's repeated threats to use chemical weapons against the Zionists, meaning Israel, and their "colonial collaborators," namely, the United States.

While strategists in Washington and elsewhere are debating the reasons for Saddam's apparent change of heart, our military in the Gulf are continuing their preparations for the day that the Iraqi leader will decide to finally play his "chemical card." Their best estimate is that the Iraqi chemical strike, when it comes, will be in the form of an artillery barrage rather than by means of missiles and will occur in response to an allied ground thrust into Kuwait. The chaos, panic, and confusion likely to result from this action will be ghastly. And not surprising! Mustard gas, Tabun, and anthrax, the most likely chemical munitions to be used by the Iraqis, kill almost as instantly as do conventional artillery, machine guns, and mortars. When skillfully used, chemical agents can be more lethal than all other forms of nonnuclear armament.

The Terrorist Threat

There is good news, too, from the antiterrorist front. Except for an isolated terrorist incident against a U.S. library in Manila that can clearly be attributed to Iraqi government direction, Saddam's terrorist organizations have not struck as yet. Perhaps our counterterrorist efforts and the relentless U.S. and allied bombing of the Iraqi command-and-control facilities have demoralized Saddam's terrorists to the point of inaction. Still, there is always the possibility that the leadership in Baghdad is holding back on its use of terror until a later, more opportune time.

The relatively few acts of terrorism that have been recorded since January 17 have been carried out by Saddam's fellow travelers, the handful of international (not Iraqi) terror organizations whose sympathies are with Saddam. Included in this group are the November 17 organization in Greece, the Abu Nidal Palestinians, and the Revolutionary Left in Turkey. Members of these organizations have been expressing their solidarity with Iraq by participating in random acts of sabotage in Europe and the Middle East, destroying cars belonging to Americans and placing bombs at American businesses, especially banks.

That Iraq has a worldwide terrorist apparatus ready to strike on signal from Baghdad can hardly be disputed. The apparatus consists of professional terrorists, disciplined and trained to carry out a variety of bombing missions, including the hijacking of aircraft and suicide attacks against civilians. When and where Saddam's terrorists will strike is anyone's guess. Persons knowledgeable in the field suggest that terrorism, being a weapon of desperation, will not be used by him until the war has entered its final stages and fortunes have turned sharply against him.

But even during periods of inaction, terror remains a major psychological threat to millions of persons. Fear of terrorism has affected the routine of most Americans, has increased tension, and has seriously depressed the travel industry. In Washington, D.C., for instance, attendance at museums, the Washington Monument, and other historical and cultural sites has dropped considerably. The Secret Service has stopped tours of the White House, and hotel and tour operators are reporting major cancellations even for the period of the Cherry Blossoms Festival when Washington is traditionally saturated with tourists. International travel has especially been affected. When, late in January 1991, the President drove to Capitol Hill to deliver his State of the Union address, security was the tightest ever. Several blocks surrounding the Capitol were cordoned off to traffic, and the few fortunate persons holding tickets to the event were required to undergo careful scrutiny at three separate security stations.

Thousands of officials, of course, in the United States and abroad, are engaged in antiterrorist activity, to include surveillance of suspects, their preemptive roundup and deportation. Many European governments have also expelled the great majority of Iraqi diplomats accredited to their countries. Terror groups do not operate in isolation. They depend on financing support and policy guidance from the governments sponsoring them. When their sponsoring diplomats are deported, terror groups lose their direction and capability to act.

Despite heightened security at home and abroad and the adoption of antiterrorist measures, Iraqi terrorists still possess the theoretical capability of striking anytime, anyplace. Experts advise against becoming paranoid over the threat, but also counsel the need for continued vigilance. Just because Saddam's terrorists have not struck as yet, does not mean that the threat of terrorism has waned.

Will There Be a Ground War?

President Bush acknowledged on February 5, 1991, that he is skeptical that air power alone can win the Gulf War. Before deciding on the timing for a ground war he is dispatching his top two military advisers to Saudi Arabia to gauge the progress of the war. A week later, after receiving reports from his Secretary of Defense and the Chairman of the Joint Chiefs of Staff, the President reported that the air campaign over Iraq and Kuwait was very, very effective. As a result he saw no need to authorize a ground offensive at this time. The President's comments came after a week of intense speculation about whether ground action would be taken to force the Iraqi forces out of their fortifications in Kuwait.

February 7, 1991

THE DEBATE OVER A JUST WAR

Addressing a joint session of Congress, thirteen days after ordering American forces into combat against Iraq, President Bush declared, "Our cause is just. Our cause is moral. Our cause is right." The United States, he noted, assumed the burden of leadership in confronting Saddam, because it is the only nation in the world with the moral standing to do so.

Is This Really a Just War?

Suddenly, theologians, politicians, and just about everybody are debating the morality of our war against Iraq. Is this truly a "just war" of "the moral equivalent of World War II," as the President asserts, or is our involvement in the Persian Gulf a mistake that is now being disguised as a moral crusade to rationalize the destruction and loss of life?

The U.S. effort to liberate Kuwait, reiterates the President, is a moral use of force and a case of good versus evil and of right versus wrong. Saddam's invasion of Kuwait is no different than Hitler's aggression against his neighbors. If it was just and moral to stop

Hitler then, it is equally just and moral to stop Saddam Hussein now. Opposed are some of the nation's leading moralists, including the U.S. Roman Catholic hierarchy and the leadership of the National Council of Churches. The war, they assert, is morally indefensible and risks violating several traditional just war criteria.

Every national leader, of course, who ever involved his nation in an armed conflict was convinced that "his" war was a "just" one. Hitler thought this when he invaded Poland, and so did President Franklin Roosevelt when he dispatched a U.S. army to free Europe from Nazism. For all we know, Saddam also considered his recent seizure of Kuwait to have been a "just" act. Whether a given war is "just" or not is a question of morality and one that the individual leader must resolve within his own conscience. There is no accepted clear-cut definition of the term. Through the ages some of the world's leading theologians and philosophers (St. Augustine and St. Thomas Aquinas among them) have been troubled by this issue and have attempted to answer it, but their efforts have fallen short of a complete answer. By using the ambiguous phrase of a "just war" to characterize Operation Desert Storm, the President has confused the debate rather than help clarify it.

Six criteria are generally used by theologians and moralists for judging a war.[3] A war to be "just" must be in response to a just cause, such as self-defense or to defeat evil; must have been declared by competent authority; must be an act of last resort, after all efforts at a peaceful settlement have failed; must have a probability of success; must be proportional (i.e., the good that will be achieved by the war must outweigh the harm); and must be "discriminate," meaning it must avoid harming noncombatants.

Reflecting briefly on the criteria above, how can one truthfully judge the launching of Operation Desert Storm on January 17 to have been an act of last resort? The President contends that extraordinary diplomatic efforts preceded hostilities. For the record, there was no senior-level diplomatic contact between the United States and Iraq during the five months preceding the war, except for the meeting in Geneva on January 12, 1991, between Secretary Baker and Iraqi Foreign Minister Aziz. That nothing of substance resulted from that meeting was hardly surprising, considering the repeated assertions by the U.S. Secretary of State that his purpose in meeting the Iraqi counterpart was "not to negotiate" but to advise him to get out of

Kuwait. The U.S. practice of dictating terms to Saddam Hussein rather than negotiating and the speed with which the economic sanctions against Iraq were judged to be ineffective hardly support the President's contention that all peaceful means had been exhausted and that the war, therefore, was unavoidable.

Future events will determine whether the good from this war will outweigh the damage done, or the degree to which the innocent have been spared the ravages of war. Even if positive assessments result from these tests, the fact that the United States failed to exhaust all peaceful alternatives before resorting to force still makes this an "unjust" war.

The First Casualty of War Is Truth

Television images from the Gulf invariably carry the caution "Cleared by U.S. Military Censors." So do live broadcasts on the conduct of the war and most newsprint stories appearing in the nation's leading newspapers. "Military censors screen pooled reports," warns the *New York Times*, meaning that some of the material included in its stories on the war may not be entirely truthful because of military censorship.

An adversarial relationship between the press and the military has always existed whenever the United States has gone to war, the press always asking for a lot of information, the military giving out far less. Never before has this relationship been more strained than in the present conflict. Largely because of the Vietnam experience and our military's belief that a hostile and unfriendly press caused the United States to "lose" that war, reporting on the Gulf is subject to the strictest rules of censorship ever imposed by our government.

Under the established press rules, visits to U.S. air, sea, and ground units in the Gulf are allowed only to designated pools of reporters, selected from among all the correspondents, photographers, and camera operators accredited to the command. But even as members of a pool, the reporters' freedom is severely restricted. They may visit only units chosen by the military, must remain at all times under the watchful eye of their military escort officers, and may talk only to individuals selected by them. All text and video and still photography resulting from such visits must first be "cleared" by the escort officers.

War correspondents not selected to participate in pools are totally frustrated in their reporting efforts. They are required to remain within the confines of their Saudi bases where their only access to war news comes from official U.S. and allied briefings.

Its rules for reporting on the war, claims the Pentagon, are not meant to silence responsible correspondents, but are designed to control the activities of a small minority of irresponsible reporters who make it a practice of reporting on the negative effects of the war and in the process influence adversely the national resolve. With nearly a thousand journalists in the area, the Pentagon says, pools are essential to manage the logistics of reporting, to protect the safety of reporters, and to discourage the flow of information that would give aid and comfort to the enemy and endanger the lives of U.S. and allied troops.

The American public is badly split on this issue. Persons supporting the war generally favor the censorship rules because they "protect" the troops. Opponents argue that the rules are nothing less than a disguised administration effort to manipulate the news from the front and to bolster popular support for the war. Correspondents assigned to the Gulf are especially critical of the rules. The military's pool system does not work, they insist, especially the requirement that all reports be cleared by military censors. The rules restrict the reporters' freedom of action and allow military sensors to eliminate anything in these reports that is critical of the military and/or the war.

That the reporters are right on this one requires little additional evidence. Since the first day of the air campaign, the news from the front has been much too clean. U.S. and allied planes leave their bases or the decks of their aircraft carriers, proceed to their targets and attack them with pinpoint accuracy, and then return home safely. Nothing is said of the human toll of these raids, or of the casualties among the civilian populations of Iraq and Kuwait. To be sure, military briefings are provided daily in Riyadh and Washington, but all of them offer no more than confusing generalizations amid stale statistics of sorties flown and Scuds fired. The officers presenting these briefings are extremely tight-lipped, dodging and evading more questions than they are actually answering. Cases of inaccurate or conflicting information abound, such as the confusion created between briefers in the Gulf and those in Washington over whether U.S. air forces had reached superiority or supremacy; what was meant with the U.S. claim that 80 percent of all sorties flown had been "effective"; or whether a building in Baghdad heavily damaged by U.S. aircraft was in fact Iraq's only factory for producing infant formula or a biological weapons plant, as claimed by the Pentagon. Were these simple inaccuracies created in the confusion of combat, or outright falsehoods conceived by overzealous supporters of the war?

"Trust me," recently pleaded General Colin Powell, the Chairman of the Joint Chiefs of Staff. Americans want to, but are troubled by his organization's apparent attempts to cast a rosy view on the events in the Gulf, rather than in providing a factual military assessment of the conflict.

Supporting the Troops but Opposing the War

They differ in age, background, and political outlook. Some are veterans of earlier peace campaigns; others are pacifists opposed to all wars; still others think the war in the Gulf is senseless and without clear objective. They all loathe Saddam Hussein and his record of brutality, but also are angry at President Bush for getting the United States involved in a catastrophic war. They are the members of America's antiwar movement.

During the long months of the summer and fall of 1990, when a military conflict with Iraq was a probability and not the reality that it is today, millions of Americans expressed skepticism over the wisdom of going to war over Kuwait. The start of the war, however, instead of strengthening the antiwar cause, has had the opposite effect. Confronted by generally positive news from the front, low casualties, and the natural tendency of Americans to rally around the flag in times of national crisis, the antiwar movement is suddenly seeing its ranks depleted. With cries of "Support the troops!" echoing across the land, few Americans are in a mood to appear unpatriotic by criticizing the President and openly opposing the war.

That the war has produced a surge of support for the President cannot be disputed. The support is there, all right, but will it persist when the one-sided high-tech air war has been replaced by the rigors and blood of a ground war? Or when the body bags begin arriving home? Or when the truth becomes known of the civilian casualties within Iraq and Kuwait as a result of the U.S. bombing?

They still march occasionally in San Francisco, in New York, and in Washington. In Lafayette Square, across from the White House, a couple of antiwar activists are pounding drums 24 hours a day, hoping that the President will hear them. The protesters are staying away from Capitol Hill, however. From the very beginning of the Gulf crisis, the Congress has tried very hard *not* to make the hard choices required of it. When it finally did take a position, it was five full months after Saddam had invaded Kuwait and the President had already deployed 400,000 troops to Saudi Arabia. The same predicament confronted the Congress then that is confronting the antiwar movement now. A "no" vote meant that the member was unpatriotic and was turning his back on the GI's at the front. Any surprise that the majority of the Congress voted yes on January 12?

The antiwar movement has learned a lot from past mistakes. Marchers carry a forest of American flags, are careful not to embrace the enemy, and in their slogans express respect and support for the troops. What inspires them to protest, they assert, is their love for America and their fear that thousands of young lives will be lost in a senseless war ("No Blood over Oil" is their slogan). The patriotic theme of their protests has caused few incidents. Even the President has been kind to the antiwar protesters--perhaps because he is so far ahead in the polls. He has no bitterness in his heart toward them, he says, nor anger at their message.

The Civilian Casualties Issue Revisited

After weeks of remaining silent on the human costs of the U.S. air raids, the government of Saddam Hussein has finally decided to speak up. The United States, it charges, is attempting to "expel Iraq from the twentieth century" by systematically destroying the nation's infrastructure, its bridges, electric power plants, and water and sewage facilities--even mosques and churches are being obliterated. U.S. aircraft are intentionally targeting Iraqi residential districts, terrorizing women and children, and killing and maiming civilians. The number of victims is estimated in the "thousands."

Is this more of Saddam Hussein's propaganda? No one knows for sure. U.S. officials concede that, considering the enormous tonnage of explosives used thus far against Iraqi military targets, some damage to civilian facilities is possible. But U.S. aircraft, they insist, are not aiming their missiles and bombs at Iraqi civilians--not intentionally that is.

The Raid on the Bomb Shelter

With hundreds of U.S. and allied planes crisscrossing the skies over Iraq and dropping "smart" and not-so-smart bombs at will, with hundreds of Tomahawk sea-launched cruise missiles raining destruction on Iraqi cities, the U.S. raid on a building in Baghdad in which hundreds of Iraqi civilians had taken refuge from the U.S. bombing was a disaster waiting to happen. In the darkness of night, on February 13, an American stealth fighter bomber dropped two laser-guided bombs on what it believed was a military command center, killing four hundred, perhaps five hundred civilians in their sleep.

"A carefully planned crime," charged the outraged Iraqis, and a "deliberate attack" against innocent civilians hiding in an air-raid shelter. The charge was instantly denied by U.S. authorities. The structure may have served once as an air-raid shelter, but it had recently been converted for military use. This had not been a bomb gone astray. The building was struck intentionally because it was on the Command's target list as an active military control center feeding instructions directly to the Iraqi war machine. If civilians happened to be inside the building (as regrettable as that may be) it was Iraq's doing, not America's.

Grisly images of charred bodies, many of young women and children, soon filled the nation's television screens. The pristine and high-tech war that Americans had been accustomed to viewing suddenly gave way to rows of corpses of innocent people, to pain and grief, and to parents in agony over the fate of their offspring. It was like the general had said on television: war is never clean; there is "collateral" damage whenever you dispatch a military force into a populated area. But to millions of Americans--especially those of the post-Korea and post-Vietnam generations--this was the first honest look at war and the devastation it causes, at the meaning of "collateral" damage, and at the cost of destroying one nation to free another.

What actually did happen? Was the structure that our stealth fighter bomber took out with such deadly accuracy a military bunker, or was the tragedy due to a misreading on our part of the building's basic purpose? Western reporters at the site overwhelmingly support the Iraqi contention. This was not a military facility, they report; there was no evidence of military equipment inside, and a sign at the building's entrance clearly identified it as a civilian air-raid shelter.

The building, retorts the Pentagon, is one of several such buildings that were built in Baghdad during the war with Iran. Recently, however, the Iraqis had added a hardened roof on the structure, painted it in camouflage colors, and brought in communications equipment. The United States has in its possession satellite photos that show military vehicles parked outside the building and men in uniform entering and leaving. The building, notes the Pentagon, is surrounded by a chain-link fence. If this was an air-raid shelter, what possible purpose could the fence serve?

The Pentagon's case appears credible, but not the carefully orchestrated public relations campaign launched by the White House. The guilty party, it implies, is Saddam Hussein himself. Please note the words of Marlin Fitzwater, the President's spokesman:

The bunker that was attacked last night was a military target, a command and control center that fed instructions directly to the Iraqi war machine. . . We have been systematically attacking these targets since the war began. We don't know why civilians were at this location. But we do know that Saddam Hussein does not share our value in the sanctity of life. Indeed, time and again he has shown willingness to sacrifice civilian lives and property to further his war aims. . . . [4]

The clear implication of the statement was that Saddam had put all these people in there with the intention of getting them killed, so that he might later charge the United States with targeting and killing innocent civilians.

The White House statement and Pentagon explanations notwithstanding, several questions still linger: When did the building become a priority military target? If it has been one all along, why was it not struck earlier in the air campaign? Why did the Command wait twenty-seven days before attacking it? And why did our satellite photos not detect the hundreds of civilians entering and leaving the building (apparently they had no difficulty recognizing men in uniform entering the building)?

What It All Will Cost

How much this war will cost is anybody's guess. The people who should know--the administration and the Pentagon--are not saying. Unofficial estimates vary, depending on one's feelings about the conflict. Persons who generally favor the war insist that its cost will be minimal ("the United States can pay it out of its hip pocket"). Opponents differ. They point at the astronomical cost of the weapons being used in the Gulf--$50 million, for instance, for an F-117 Stealth aircraft; over $1 million for each Patriot anti-missile missile--amid predictions of dire consequences for the economy and the federal budget deficit should the war last long.

The Congressional Budget Office has come the closest of anyone in official Washington to providing us with a considered estimate of the war's cost. A "short" war, it says, lasting no more than one month should cost about $28 billion; a long war, of up to six months duration, $86 billion. The ultimate cost would depend on two factors: the war's duration and the extent to which future Congresses will elect to replace all or a part of the ammunition and equipment expended during the course of the fighting.

Political considerations, of course, are behind the administration's absolute silence on this issue. Announcing a price tag on the war would not only imply U.S. government confidence on the length of the fighting, which it obviously does not have, but also would require it to announce a politically explosive decision on the war's financing, namely, whether by new taxes, a surtax, or by borrowing. To be sure, some of America's allies (Saudi Arabia, Kuwait, Japan, Germany, and others) have already pledged nearly $30 billion toward the war's costs, but how many of these pledges will later translate into hard cash remains to be seen.

This entire matter of foreigners paying Americans to fight the war has left many at home totally perplexed. To many, the arrangement smacks of a "mercenary" deal: they pay, we fight for them. Still others find the image of Uncle Sam--hat in hand and begging for funds--to be downright embarrassing, undignified, and degrading. Many complain that the allied contributions are small and totally out of line with the sacrifices that the United States is prepared to make. The administration is well aware of these feelings, which explains the increasing tempo of its fund-raising efforts among the allies. A fair distribution of costs for the war, it reminds Tokyo and Bonn, especially, is for the allies to pay 80 percent of the costs and for the United States to pay the balance.

Each bomb dropped or missile fired at Iraqi targets is sharply increasing the cost of the war. That the ultimate price Americans will have to pay will be determined by Saddam's bullheadedness and our allies' erratic behavior is hardly reassuring.

NOTES

1. William H. Honan, "Attacks on Iraq Worry and Divide Archaeologists," *New York Times*, February 9, 1991.

2. Patrick E. Tyler, "Pentagon Said to Authorize U.S. Use of Nonlethal Gas," *New York Times*, January 26, 1991.

3. Richard N. Ostling, "A Just Conflict, or Just a Conflict?" *Time*, February 11, 1991; Jeffery L. Sheler et al., "Holy War Doctrines," *U.S. News and World Report*, February 11, 1991.

4. The White House, "Statement on Bombing of Building in Iraq," by Marlin Fitzwater, February 13, 1991.

3 Diplomacy Aborted Again

APPREHENSION OVER A PREMATURE CEASE-FIRE

Less than three weeks into the air campaign, Washington once again was confronted with the issue of war or peace when a number of nonaligned nations began exploring the possibility for a cease-fire. Their efforts could not have been more untimely or inopportune. With the air battle going better than expected and the U.N. coalition holding strong, the United States was in no mood to end the war. To no one's surprise, Washington threw cold water on any and all peace overtures, pointedly turning its back on any arrangement that might suggest a U.S. willingness to "negotiate" a solution to the crisis with Saddam Hussein.

Washington's principal concern, of course, was with the Iraqi army, which thus far had escaped the brunt of the war. It simply made no sense, Washington reasoned, to accept a cease-fire now and in the process give Saddam Hussein the opportunity to retrieve his army from Kuwait, regroup it, and then return to threaten his neighbors. Stopping the war before Iraq's military machine had been totally destroyed--especially its army--was one option Washington did not wish to entertain.

Under the circumstances, the United States felt no compunction about telling all bearers of cease-fire proposals that it was not interested. There was one aspect, however, in this exercise of peacemaking and negotiation that began to trouble Washington. Increasingly, Moscow was becoming involved in the peace movement, with the distinct possibility that in the near future, it too might launch a cease-fire plan calling for a premature end to the fighting. The threat of a Soviet peace plan haunted Washington policymakers throughout the air war nearly as much as did the so-called doomsday scenario, namely, the possibility that Saddam Hussein might suddenly order his army out of Kuwait, before the United States had a chance to deal with it. American diplomacy worked extremely hard to keep Moscow tightly within the U.N. coalition and to prevent it from sponsoring a peace plan, even sacrificing in the process its long-standing policy goal for the liberation of the Baltic states.

January 29 to February 9, 1991

The Peace Offer That Was Not

One of the earliest indications of Washington's disdain for ending the war by means of a diplomatic initiative occurred late in January, on the very day that President Bush was scheduled to deliver his annual State of the Union message to the Congress and the nation. In his limousine en route to Capitol Hill on the evening of January 29, President Bush was shown the text of a communiqué that Secretary of State James Baker and then Soviet Foreign Minister Alexander Bessmertnykh had signed a few hours earlier at the conclusion of their three-day talks in Washington, D.C. By all accounts, the President definitely did not like what he read.

To be sure, nothing in the communiqué departed from previous U.S. policy statements on Iraq and the war (see Appendix E). But the context in which the various American positions were stated seemed to convey the impression that Washington was offering Iraq a link between withdrawal from Kuwait and a settlement of the Palestinian-Israeli conflict. (It will be recalled that from the outset President Bush had steadfastly opposed the linking of these two issues.) The communiqué also advised Iraq that the United States was not seeking its destruction and that all hostilities would cease when "Iraq made an unequivocal commitment to withdraw from Kuwait . . . backed by immediate concrete steps leading to full compliance with the Security Council resolutions." The statement also promised a Soviet role in the postwar arrangements in the Gulf and a redoubling of efforts to resolve the broader Middle East issues.

As joint statements from the foreign secretaries of the two superpowers go, the communiqué of January 29 was odd indeed. For one, it was prepared, signed, and released without the President's knowledge or even that of his adviser for National Security Affairs. Once the communiqué had been signed, a copy was posted in the Department of State press room but no distribution was made to the waiting reporters. It was the Soviet Foreign Minister who let the cat out of the bag. After signing the document, he rushed before the television cameras to read selected excerpts from it. When word of the communiqué reached Jerusalem, the government of Israel was stunned. Decisions were being made in Washington, it protested, affecting the state of Israel without consulting first with its leadership. Israel, emphasized its Foreign Ministry spokesman, would oppose any settlement that left Saddam Hussein in power. Confusion and questions also met the communiqué's publication in Paris, Rome, and Bonn. But in Moscow, the agreement was hailed as a significant shift in U.S. position and an "important" document, with the Kremlin especially pleased with its new role in the Middle East.

What had gone wrong? Nothing, really. The war was going well and the U.S. government saw no reason to want to negotiate with Iraq. The entire matter of the communiqué was just another demonstration of Washington's continued effort to keep the Soviet Union tied to the anti-Iraq coalition and to prevent it from floating a peace plan of its own. In the week prior to the Baker-Bessmertnykh meeting, Moscow had suddenly become extremely critical of the conduct of the war, especially the destruction suffered by many residential areas in Iraq as a result of the allied bombing. The criticism of the United States had reached a crescendo, especially among Soviet hardliners and the military. The United States, they charged, had rushed into the war and had not allowed sanctions sufficient time to work.

In Washington, the Bush administration spent the next few days trying to squelch rumors of a policy change. The communiqué, it said repeatedly, was not designed to announce a new U.S. policy, but merely to assure the Soviet Union that the destruction of Iraq was not official policy and that Moscow, in recognition of its faithful membership in the U.N. coalition, would be part of the postwar arrangements on the Middle East. (This, of course, had been a long-standing foreign policy goal of Moscow but one that had eluded it through the years.) Even the State Department joined the effort to defame its communiqué. It was a routine statement, it said defensively, that had been widely and wildly misinterpreted by the media. There had been no change in America's position, and definitely no invitation had been extended to Iraq to negotiate the future of Kuwait by linking it to the Palestinian problem.

The Iranians as Peacemakers

The furor over the U.S.-Soviet communiqué had hardly died down when Iran, Iraq's archenemy and next-door neighbor, suddenly began hinting at peacemaking. Iran, of course, had its own reasons for wanting to play peacemaker, but the fact that it did want to become involved in the thankless process aroused enormous interest. Within hours of Teheran's official announcement, visitors from Turkey, France, India, and the Soviet Union converged on Teheran to hear more about the Iranian plan and to explore its prospects for success. For its part, Washington yawned, displaying even less enthusiasm for Teheran's efforts than it had shown for France's earlier attempts to end the dispute over Kuwait by means of a diplomatic initiative.

The Iranian peace initiative received its initial impetus with the arrival in Teheran, on January 31, of Saadoun Hammadi, then Iraq's Deputy Prime Minister. Ostensibly, Hammadi's visit was for the purpose of reviewing with the Iranian authorities the fate of the Iraqi aircraft that had taken refuge on Iranian soil. But on arrival in Teheran the Iraqi official suggested that the purpose of his visit was much broader. He had come to brief the Iranian leadership, he noted, on the course of the war and was carrying with him a message from Saddam Hussein to Iranian President Ali Akbar Hashemi Rafsanjani.

To Washington, Hammadi's words sounded like another Iraqi overture to Iran to abandon its neutrality and to join the war on its side. This was not the first time Saddam had tried to get into the good graces of his more powerful neighbor. Early on in his confrontation with the United States, the Iraqi leader had returned to Iran all prisoners of war (POWs) held by Iraq and had withdrawn his troops from Iranian territory seized during the eight-year war. True, Iran had denounced Iraq's aggression in Kuwait and had promised to honor the sanctions imposed by the United Nations, but it had also condemned bitterly the military buildup of the U.S. and European military forces in the Gulf. It was in the latter connection that Saddam saw hope for an Iranian policy reversal.

The Iranian peace initiative was unveiled on February 3 with an announcement by President Rafsanjani that his nation had presented to Hammadi during his visit in Teheran certain "ideas" for ending the war. If Baghdad's response to these ideas were positive, he noted, he himself would be prepared to meet with Saddam and also with representatives from Washington to pursue the initiative. Rafsanjani did not divulge details on the specific ideas that he had communicated to Iraq, but his plan reportedly called for a three-step process for resolving the Kuwait crisis. As a first step, Iran's spiritual leader would make an appeal to all sides to cease the fighting, Iraq would withdraw from Kuwait, and so would the U.S. and European forces stationed in the Gulf region. As a second step, a number of face-saving enticements would be initiated, such as the creation of an Islamic force to police the border between Iraq and Kuwait, review by Islamic experts of the territorial disputes in the area, and creation of an Islamic fund to provide financing for repairing the war damage inflicted on Iraq. A nonaggression pact among the nations of the Gulf region would be the final step in the peace process.

As expected, the United States reacted coolly to Iran's diplomatic maneuvering. "There is nothing to negotiate with Iraq," noted Margaret Tutwilder, spokesperson for the Department of State. Her boss, Secretary of State James Baker, was equally direct when asked about the Iranian initiative. Iran, he noted, has conducted itself in a very credible manner throughout the war, "but we do not seek its mediation in the conflict." Behind the statements was, of course, Washington's resolve not to end the fighting until the Iraqi war machine had been totally destroyed, as well as an inherent mistrust of the Iranians, dating back to the days of the taking of the U.S. hostages in Teheran by Islamic fundamentalists.

As it turned out, on February 9, in one of his many senseless and outright foolish decisions on the conduct of the war, Saddam closed the door to Iran's diplomatic initiative, ruling out any compromise on Kuwait and declaring his intention to go on with the conflict. Kuwait was not the issue, he declared defiantly, but attempts by the United States and its allies to destroy Iraq were. Saddam's rejection of Iran's peace initiative made the purpose of Hammadi's trip to Teheran all too apparent. Iraq had hoped that its senior official would lure Iran into the war on its side, not act as an intermediary for surrendering Kuwait to the United States.

February 15, 1991

Saddam's Hoax

Yet, less than a week after he had summarily rejected the Iranian peace initiative and had promised to go on with the war, Saddam Hussein switched signals and began promoting a peace initiative of his own. The reasons for his apparent change of heart should be obvious. Iran and Israel--the two nations whose entry into the war would have gravely complicated the conflict--refused to be dragged into the fighting, the U.N. coalition (especially its Arab members) was holding strong, and Iraq's military machine was taking an unmerciful beating at the hands of the U.S. Air Force. Worse yet, a deadly ground war was about to be launched by the coalition, foreboding nothing but doom for Baghdad's demoralized and ill-equipped ground forces. The need for the fighting to end was so clear, even Saddam came to realize it.

The Iraqi leader's peace plan, when it was announced in the morning hours of February 15, caused a global sensation, giving hope for a brief moment that the senseless fighting would soon be terminated. But the peace plan included also a lot of fine print and a long list of "conditions" that the Iraqi leader foolishly, but in typical Middle Eastern bargaining fashion, attached to his plan (see Appendix F).

Iraq, said, the announcement from Baghdad, was prepared to "deal" with Security Council Resolution 660 of 1990 with the aim of reaching an honorable and acceptable political solution to the crisis, including withdrawal, if certain conditions were met. The conditions were a mix of old and new and included several demands included in an earlier (August 12, 1990) Iraqi peace plan. The conditions were so heavily slanted in favor of Iraq that, had the United States and its allies agreed to them, Saddam would have exited the Gulf war as the ultimate victor. The question logically arises: in view of his hopeless military situation, did the Iraqi leader really believe that he could dictate terms or that anyone would take them seriously? Not really! Saddam never expected his conditions to provide the basis for a diplomatic arrangement, or to be anything more than an opening bid in a protracted negotiating session with the United States from which to salvage something from the war. But, sadly for the thousands who lost their lives in the subsequent fighting, President Bush and most other leaders of the U.N. coalition refused to see the "conditions" for what they really were--opening bids in a protracted bargaining session. Instead they focused on them, made them the centerpiece of the Iraqi leader's plan, and ultimately rejected the plan because of them.

There were essentially nine "conditions" in Saddam's peace plan, ranging from demands that the United Nations abrogate all its resolutions against Iraq, including its global economic embargo and resolutions holding Iraq liable for war damages and economic losses because of the crisis, to a call that Israel withdraw from Palestine and all other Arab territories it is now occupying, to a demand for the withdrawal from the region of all U.S. and allied military forces, including the U.S. naval and air forces stationed in the Gulf for years. In return for these concessions, Saddam promised to "deal" with U.N. Resolution 660--not to actually comply with it. Resolution 660, it will be remembered, demanded Iraq's unconditional withdrawal from Kuwait.

Why should anyone take these terms seriously? President Bush and several other leaders of the U.N. coalition did, not because of naiveté, but because Saddam's conditions offered them a tailor-made excuse for rejecting the plan and for continuing with the war. The President was well aware that Saddam Hussein was hurting and that his war machine was near collapse. Estimates from the front on the day that Saddam floated his offer showed Iraqi losses to include a total of 1,300 tanks, 1,000 pieces of artillery, and 50,000 troops. By offering to "deal" with the U.N. resolution on Kuwait, the Iraqi leader was signaling his defeat at the hands of the U.S. forces and his readiness to withdraw from the occupied lands. But the President was adamant. Negotiations and a diplomatic arrangement had no place until the total military defeat of Iraq had been accomplished, or at least until the Iraqi leader had been forced to accept a humiliating withdrawal from Kuwait.

The plan is a "hoax," charged President Bush within hours of hearing the Iraqi plan (see Appendix G). Promises would not suffice.

Until Saddam actually began a massive withdrawal from Kuwait, the coalition forces would continue their efforts to force compliance with all U.N. resolutions. Underlying the President's hard line was suspicion that the Iraqi leader's initiative had the potential for dividing the international coalition. With the Soviet Union sliding back to the Cold War era and its military demanding that the Soviet-Iraqi relationship be preserved, with Iran considering the United States as big a Satan as Saddam, and with China and France uncertain, there was a strong basis for the President's fears. The plan, after all, had come less than forty-eight hours after the U.S. bombing of a civilian air-raid shelter in Baghdad, at which reportedly over four hundred Iraqis had perished. Iraq had reaped enormous propaganda gains from the event, with millions of people around the world seeing pictures of broken bodies caused by American smart bombs and wondering why a cease-fire was not being negotiated.

With the President pouring cold water on the Saddam initiative, the Iraqi leader's offer to "deal" with U.N. Resolution 660 went nowhere. The proposal was a bogus sham, noted British Prime Minister John Major. "Not serious," agreed the Arab governments in the allied coalition. As for Israel, it dismissed the Iraqi statement outright. "Israel," said a senior adviser to Prime Minister Yitzhak Shamir, "would find unacceptable any arrangement that leaves Saddam Hussein in power." The only statement supporting the Iraqi initiative came from Moscow, with Foreign Minister Alexander Bessmertnykh calling Iraq's decision to discuss a possible withdrawal from Kuwait encouraging. The proposal, he noted, opens a new chapter in the history of the Persian Gulf. But then, as we shall discuss later, Moscow had its own agenda to pursue.

Ironically, Saddam's peace initiative of February 15, 1991, will be remembered in history less for what the Iraqi leader said than for four words spoken by our President. It was in reaction to Saddam's peace initiative that President Bush made his now famous statement of encouragement to the Iraqi people to overthrow Saddam Hussein, which later provided the basis for the Shiite and Kurdish revolts. Said the President: "But there's another way for the bloodshed to stop, and that is for the Iraqi military *and the Iraqi people* to take matters into their own hands to force Saddam Hussein the dictator to step aside."[1] A few weeks later, the Iraqi people did take matters into their hands, and disaster followed. But more on this later.

February 11 to 22, 1991

Gorbachev and His Shifting Agenda

Washington's worst fears, the prospect of Moscow becoming actively engaged as a peace broker of the Persian Gulf war before Iraq's war machine had been totally destroyed and humiliated, began to take shape on February 11 when Yevgeni Primakov, President Gorbachev's Middle East adviser, arrived in Baghdad. It was not the first time that Moscow had involved its senior diplomat in trying to resolve the Kuwait crisis. Primakov had spent most of October 1990 traveling back and forth between Baghdad, Moscow, London, and Washington in a highly visible but futile search for a diplomatic arrangement designed to bring about Iraq's withdrawal from Kuwait, but also to set the stage for a postwar settlement of the Arab-Israeli and Palestinian issues.

Two reasons, of course, accounted for Moscow's yearning to become the arbiter of a Persian Gulf peace: expectation that enormous strategic benefits and influence would result for the Soviet Union by bartering a Middle East settlement, and an obvious desire to protect Iraq from further annihilation in the hands of the U.S. military. Iraq, after all, was not just another Arab nation. For years it had served as the Soviet Union's principal ally in the Arab world, buying its arms and providing Moscow with much-needed hard currency. By interceding on behalf of beleaguered Iraq at this critical juncture, Moscow hoped that its strategic relationship with the oil-rich country would survive and that Iraq would again resume its role as Moscow's principal client in the Arab world and its largest and best arms buyer.

Technically at least, the Soviet Union had been a member of the U.N. coalition throughout the war, but its affinity toward its old friend and ally, Iraq, could hardly be concealed. The Soviet Union refused to provide military troops or financial contributions for prosecuting the war and cast its votes on the U.N. resolutions condemning Iraq's occupation of Kuwait, very, very reluctantly-- especially the vote on Resolution 678, which authorized the use of force. Despite Iraq's violation of Kuwait, the Soviet Union maintained intact its treaty of friendship and cooperation with Iraq, working behind the scenes to support its former ally and keeping a respectable distance from Washington's military moves. On February 9, 1991, for instance, Moscow warned the U.S.-led alliance against exceeding the United Nations mandate. Any political settlement of the war, it warned, would also have to include the issue of the Arab-Israeli conflict. The latter comment, of course, reflected one of Saddam's long-standing demands for ending the Kuwait crisis.

A number of issues made the latest round of Soviet diplomacy especially worrisome to Washington. For one, with the resignation of Foreign Minister Shevardnadze and the increasing presence at the Soviet Foreign Ministry of hardline Communists, the United States could no longer be certain where Gorbachev stood on the basic issues of the Gulf war. To be sure, the Soviet leader had met President Bush in Helsinki on September 9, 1990, and had agreed with him on the need to reverse Iraq's invasion of Kuwait. But did the Soviet leader hold the same views five months later? Could he possibly be pursuing now a pro-Iraqi diplomatic initiative as proof to Soviet hardliners of his loyalty to Iraq, the former ally? Any thoughts that the Soviet leader was not sincere in his quest for a nonmilitary end to the war disappeared on February 11, when Gorbachev petitioned President Bush to delay the start of the ground offensive by a few days so that he might be able to barter a deal. With credentials on both sides, Gorbachev's ability to "cut" such a deal was real. To Washington, determined to charge full steam ahead with the task of destroying Iraq's military machine, the actions of the Soviet leader were not only unnecessary but outright suspect.

On Gorbachev's instructions, Primakov began his diplomatic initiative in Baghdad by offering Saddam Hussein a fairly simple and straightforward proposal (not at all pro-Iraqi, as Washington had feared). Iraq, he suggested, should announce the total withdrawal of its troops from Kuwait, make the offer without conditions, and establish as short a deadline as possible for the withdrawal. It is important to remember that the Primakov proposal was made on February 12, three days *after* Saddam had rejected a much more favorable proposal by Iran, but three days *before* Saddam's own peace plan of February 15 (the "hoax"). Saddam did not reject Primakov's proposal outright, but asked instead a number of questions. What guarantees were there that the Iraqi soldiers leaving Kuwait would not be attacked? Would the allied bombing of Iraq stop? Would the U.N. sanctions against Iraq be lifted?[2] Primakov, of course, was unable to answer these questions without extensive shuttle diplomacy between Washington, Baghdad, Moscow, and New York. But first, he had to have a tentative approval of his package by Saddam, which the Iraqi leader refused to give. The most that Primakov could get out of Saddam was that "Iraq's national leadership was studying the Soviet proposal." Three days later Saddam announced his own peace proposal (the "hoax"), only to have it summarily rejected by President Bush. How much Primakov's proposal had influenced the formulation of the Iraqi peace plan of February 15 will never be known.

The President's rejection of Saddam's February 15 proposal left the Soviet Union holding the only viable plan for ending the Gulf war. So on to Moscow flew Iraqi Foreign Minister Tariq Aziz on February 17 in the hope of salvaging what he could from a totally hopeless situation. The first Aziz-Gorbachev meeting was held on the morning of February 18. It was followed by a return flight to Baghdad by Aziz for consultations, and a second round of talks with the Soviet leader in Moscow three days later. The February 18 Aziz-Gorbachev talks focused essentially on the same Soviet package that Primakov had offered Saddam Hussein a week earlier. No one knows for sure what additional incentives were added by Moscow to induce Iraq's acceptance of the plan. In line with their usual practice in diplomatic negotiations, the Soviets were playing their cards extremely close to the vest (President Bush was briefed on the proceedings, but reportedly was asked to keep them "confidential," which he did.) In the press there was speculation, however, that the Soviet package included also pledges to Iraq that the broader Middle East problems, meaning the Arab-Israeli dispute and the Palestinian issue, would be addressed once the Gulf war had ended; that the territorial integrity of Iraq and Saddam's personal safety would be respected; and that the international economic sanctions against Iraq would be lifted. According to Primakov, who was present at the February 18 talks, President Gorbachev offered also a pledge to Aziz that Iraq's troops departing Kuwait would not be "shot in the back."

The Gorbachev package confronted President Bush with an awful predicament. Instead of a pro-Iraqi deal, which he had suspected Moscow would come up with and which would have been easy for him to reject, the Soviet leader had produced a package that even administration officials agreed was reasonable. To be sure, there were in the package also all those pledges to Iraq that the United States opposed, but technically these were Soviet pledges, not U.S. or U.N. pledges, and therefore would have no binding force on the U.S. government. The doomsday scenario began to haunt Washington once again. What if Saddam suddenly accepted the Soviet proposal? How could President Bush order a ground offensive, in light of Iraq's readiness to comply with the basic terms of the coalition? How could he risk lives to liberate Kuwait, when a peaceful Iraqi withdrawal was imminent at the small price of some Soviet promises that were not binding on the United States anyway?[3]

After a quick trip back to Baghdad, presumably for the purpose of clearing the Gorbachev package with the Iraqi national leadership, Iraqi Foreign Minister Aziz returned to Moscow near midnight on February 21. Time was of the essence, so he was driven from the airport directly to the Kremlin where a waiting Gorbachev wanted to know the Iraqi response. Iraq will accept Resolution 660, announced Aziz, and is prepared to remove its troops from Kuwait, but it needs time to do so. Judging from the jubilant mood of Vitaly Ignatenko, Gorbachev's spokesman, when he appeared before the international press corps to announce the news, it was precisely what Moscow had hoped to hear. The response from Baghdad is positive, declared Ignatenko, unable to contain his enthusiasm, and "it is possible to find a way out of the military conflict in the Gulf along the following lines." He then proceeded to read the points agreed to between President Gorbachev and Iraqi Foreign Minister Aziz.

Washington officialdom read the transcript of the statement very, very carefully. It contained many of the provisions Washington had been demanding--Iraqi withdrawal from Kuwait, the release of POWs--but there were also numerous omissions in the plan, as well as four provisions that read like Iraqi "conditions" or "terms." Among the latter was the provision for the lifting of all U.N. economic sanctions on Iraq once two-thirds of its forces had withdrawn from Kuwait, and the removal of all remaining U.N. resolutions after the troop withdrawal had been completed. In a switch that pleased Washington, the Gorbachev plan said nothing of a Middle East peace conference or of the need to settle the Israeli-Arab conflict after the war.

While official Washington was scrutinizing the Gorbachev-Aziz transcript, a formal telephone call was placed by the Kremlin to the White House. It was about 3 a.m. Moscow time (February 22) and about 7 p.m. Washington time (February 21) when the two leaders finally spoke. According to the Soviet version of the call, President Bush "expressed appreciation for Mr. Gorbachev's efforts" but voiced doubts that the change in Baghdad's position would lead to anything. The U.S. President, notes Yevgeni Primakov, who was present while the call was being made, was especially "dissatisfied with the period set for the troop withdrawal."[4] The U.S. version of the call is considerably different. According to Marlin Fitzwater, the White House spokesman, President Bush told his Soviet counterpart that he had serious concerns about several points in the plan, but that he would examine the plan anyway.

To President Bush, bent on destroying the Iraqi military machine and humiliating its leader, the Soviet leader's peace initiative was beginning to get out of control. Events in Moscow no longer left any doubt. Mikhail Gorbachev was not merely going through the motions in the hope of gathering international accolades. He was determined to end the war and arrange a peaceful solution to the crisis, no matter what. And to the surprise of Washington, the Soviet leader was playing the game according to the rules, listening to both sides, probing for areas of agreement or accommodation, and being especially sensitive to America's demands. It all would have been perfectly agreeable, had it not been for the fact that Gorbachev's goal--salvaging Saddam and his army--was diametrically opposed to the American objective.

Reports from Moscow that the Gorbachev-Aziz talks were continuing made Washington even more wary. At the suggestion of the Soviet leader, the talks next shifted to three issues of priority concern to the Americans: (1) the timing for the release of the allied POWs; (2) how much time to allow the Iraqis for evacuating Kuwait (Baghdad was asking for six weeks; the United States would agree to no more than four days, in the hope of forcing Iraq to leave behind as much of its equipment as possible); and (3) the need for the Iraqi authorities to disclose the location of all land and sea mines in the Kuwait theater of operations. Of the three issues, the toughest to resolve was the timing for Iraqi withdrawal. The more time allowed to Iraq to clear its military forces from Kuwait, the more equipment and munitions it would be able to withdraw. The goal of the U.S. military, needless to say, was to deny Saddam's troops as much of their armaments as possible, especially the hundreds of tanks that they had converted into artillery pieces by concealing them deep under the Kuwaiti sand.

The only way, Washington reasoned, to put an end to the Soviet initiative without outright offense to Soviet President Gorbachev was to gloss over the progress made by the Soviet leader and to focus instead on the issues still remaining to be settled. Behind this strategy was the hope that international criticism of the package in its present form would force the Soviet leader to continue talking to the Iraqis, thus forestalling the plan's presentation to the U.N. Security Council for approval.

The Soviet plan (see Appendix H) falls short in a number of ways, charged the President's men in unison on February 22, because it represents a conditional withdrawal, while the United Nations resolutions call for Iraq to leave Kuwait unconditionally.[5] Others asserted that Saddam was not really serious about leaving Kuwait. The Iraqi leader was using the Soviet peace plan as a ploy to delay indefinitely the launching of the U.S. ground offensive. Singled out for criticism were provisions in the Gorbachev plan that would have required the lifting of economic and other sanctions imposed upon Iraq by the United Nations. Canceling these resolutions would allow Baghdad to escape payment of reparations for the damage caused Kuwait during its occupation. And just in case the Soviet leader had plans to surprise the United States by forcing his plan on the U.N. Security Council, critics noted that the sanctions imposed by the Security Council could only be lifted by a new vote of the council where the United States and its allies (the United Kingdom and France) were holding the power of veto.

As far as official Washington was concerned, the Gorbachev peace plan died on February 22, when President Bush issued his "final ultimatum" to Saddam Hussein, demanding that he withdraw his forces from Kuwait beginning at noon on Saturday, February 23. But in Moscow, the Soviet-Iraqi dialogue continued, with the Soviets persisting to do much of America's bidding. Several hours *after* the U.S. deadline had passed but *before* the President had ordered the troops to launch their ground offensive, Iraq agreed to the immediate and unconditional withdrawal of its armed forces from Kuwait but pointedly made the announcement in Moscow as part of the Gorbachev initiative. (Whether Iraq agreed also at that time to comply fully with all applicable U.N. resolutions is unclear.) The Soviet leader immediately notified the U.N. Security Council requesting that an emergency session of the Council be held to combine into one package the U.S. demands and the plan accepted by Iraq. The two sides, the Soviet President declared, were not so far apart as to justify the escalation of the war by launching a ground offensive. But at 10 p.m. EST on the same evening President Bush ordered the start of the ground war. Perhaps as many as 100,000 Iraqi soldiers lost their lives, and thousands others were maimed for life by the advancing allied forces, as a result of the rush to war and the President's refusal to give diplomacy one last chance to resolve the issue peacefully.

February 15 to 22, 1991

THE ENDGAME

Wanted: A Victory on the Battlefield

Millions of Americans of course were puzzled, even distressed, by the President's rejection of the Soviet diplomatic initiative. The Moscow package, after all, did offer what they understood to be the basic purpose for their nation's involvement in the Gulf--the withdrawal of Iraq from Kuwait. So why the rejection?

The President's determination to humiliate Iraq militarily before agreeing to a cease-fire raised serious questions about the real purpose for America's presence in the region. Had the destruction of Saddam's war machine, not merely the removal of his troops from Kuwait, suddenly become the essential precondition for peace in the Gulf? On what authority?

Beyond the U.S. borders, too, there was disbelief and frustration over the President's rejection of the Soviet initiative. Why reject the option of a cease-fire, wondered U.S. friends and foes alike (especially in the Middle East and in Western Europe), and in the process run the risk of a destructive war and the likelihood of a destabilized Middle East? What possible harm could come from pausing momentarily to explore the chances for ending the bloodshed? The war was essentially over and Saddam had been defeated. The world knew it, and the Iraqi leader himself knew it. He would not have made his offer of February 15 (the "hoax") or sent his

Foreign Minister rushing to Moscow were it not for this fact. Saddam had nothing to gain by continuing the war, except to heap more harm and devastation on his nation and on his defeated army. Rhetoric and negotiating gyrations aside, the Iraqi leader was ready to throw in the towel and was looking to his friends in Moscow to finalize the arrangements of surrender and spare him the embarrassment of a devastating defeat.

By his unyielding insistence that Iraq comply unconditionally with all twelve U.N. resolutions and his obvious preference for ending the war on the battlefield rather than on the diplomatic table, the President elected to ignore the desperate military situation confronting Iraq at the time. The helpless nation of 17 million had taken a terrible beating at the hands of the U.N. coalition. It had been isolated internationally and was growing weaker with each passing day. Its nuclear weapons program lay in ruins, as did its chemical and biological weapons-making facilities. Its army in Kuwait was on the verge of collapse, yet the President was acting as if it still represented a military force that had to be reckoned with. Critics, perplexed by the President's logic, wondered: Why continue with the war and the uncertainties that it entailed, when the other side had already expressed readiness to surrender? Of what military value would be the continued pounding of the already beaten Iraqi army? Why embitter the Arab world by rejecting a diplomatic arrangement that had the potential for developing lasting solutions to the region's problems? Why the emphasis on a U.S. victory on the battlefield, when the region's most divisive problems--the Arab-Israeli-Palestinian conflict and the proliferation of weapons of mass destruction-- required regional as opposed to American solutions?

In retrospect, it is clear that U.S. acceptance of the Moscow initiative would have served America's interests in a number of ways. It would have avoided an unnecessary ground war and spared the lives of thousands on both sides of the conflict, it would have achieved the U.S. objective of forcing Saddam to leave Kuwait, and it would have preserved the U.S.-Soviet relationship at a very critical juncture of its history. Yes, Moscow would have reaped diplomatic benefits in the process; it would have been foolish not to expect to. The Soviet Union could not remain a disinterested bystander in a major war fought near its borders, especially in one where Muslims bore the brunt of the suffering. Muslims, after all, represent a sizeable minority within the Soviet Union and one whose interests Moscow could not afford to ignore.

The Nation Ponders a Ground War

The decision on the next stage of the war, whether to continue with the air campaign alone or to launch a ground offensive to forcibly dislodge Saddam's forces from Kuwait, preoccupied the national psyche during much of February 1991. The issue proved extremely divisive, splitting traditional allies and blurring the lines between hawks and doves, supporters and opponents of the President's war policies. Underlying the national debate were two judgments: a strictly military one on the ability of air power alone to bring about the defeat of Saddam Hussein's army, especially of the 150,000 or so Republican Guards entrenched in Kuwait and in southern Iraq, and an equally important political judgment relating to a host of war-related domestic and international issues.

The political judgment was the President's alone to make. Electing to delay a ground offensive ran the risk of the Soviet Union or some other nation sympathetic to Iraq pursuing a peace plan designed to rescue the Iraqi military, possibly even raising Saddam to hero status in the eyes of the Islamic world for having successfully confronted the combined military forces of nearly thirty nations. A delay could also strain the U.N. coalition, causing members at the margin (Syria and Egypt?) to drop out and neutral states (Iran and Jordan?) to assume an increasingly anti-American stance. At the opposite end of the spectrum, rushing into a ground war and attacking the Iraqi defenses--too soon or in the wrong places--could cause the President enormous harm, both politically and internationally. The high troop casualties expected from a ground war were certain to decrease the President's popularity at home and to diminish congressional support for the war effort.

The dilemma was hardly new. It first surfaced when the President in November 1990 ordered a major troop buildup in the area, including the deployment of ground forces capable of "offensive" missions. It persisted throughout the air campaign, despite assurances by the administration that the United States would not allow itself to be provoked into a ground war prematurely and that the bombing of

Iraqi targets would continue until the air strikes had totally weakened Saddam's war machine. The official assurances notwithstanding, the national anxiety over the likelihood of a ground offensive remained alive, fueled by recurring warnings by persons close to the war effort that the air strikes alone were not proving sufficient to nudge the Iraqi forces out of their fortified trenches.

The prospect of a "bloody and ugly" land war once again energized the nation's war opposition. Speaking out against the planned expansion of the conflict, the voices of American pacifists were not alone. Joining them this time around were a great many hawks, well-informed and discerning supporters of the President who for reasons of national strategy opposed a ground offensive, or at least hoped that it would be delayed until the very end. With the air campaign going so well, they wondered, why even consider a ground offensive? Given enough time and patience air power could win the war. Why expose the U.S. troops to the dangers of chemical weapons, mines, and the well-entrenched Iraqi artillery, when air and naval power alone could get the job done? Saddam Hussein desperately wanted the United States to start a ground engagement. Why accommodate him by fighting on the battlefield of his choice and under conditions familiar to his troops? By shifting from the certainties of the air war to the uncertain terrain of ground combat, the United States was running the risk of increased casualties and the possibility of the war getting out of control. Cut off the Iraqis from their food, fuel, and water supplies, they implored the President; keep up the merciless air and naval bombardment of front-line troops; pulverize their lines of communication and storage depots. The Iraqis would have no choice but to surrender. As one nationally syndicated writer so cleverly put it, "The time to contemplate a ground war is when the air war is doing nothing more than making the [Iraqi] rubble bounce."[6]

Before long, domestic politics and service infighting began to influence the national decision on the ground war. With Saddam hanging on the ropes, the result primarily of Air Force and Navy bombing missions, supporters of the Army and of the Marine Corps began actively campaigning for "ground action," presumably so that Army and Marine forces would also share in the glory of victory. In a world of shrinking defense dollars and competing military missions, it was essential for the Army and the Marine Corps to get equal billing in Saddam's crushing defeat, along with the Navy and the Air

Force.

Not surprisingly, persons with strong Army and Marine ties were at the forefront of the call for an early ground offensive. A ground war is inevitable, they argued. No war has ever been won from the air and neither will this one. Aircraft can destroy bridges and tunnels; they can cripple telecommunications facilities, nuclear laboratories, and chemical production plants; but they can never be effective against men and materiel hidden under thick tiers of sand. The only way to take out the entrenched Iraqi soldiers in Kuwait would be for the Army and the Marines to charge across enemy territory, surround the fortified positions, and force the Iraqi troops into the open where they would be easier targets for American and allied close-air support aircraft.

The Battlefield Is Ready

On February 19, in one of his periodic updates to the nation and the world on the progress of the war, General Schwarzkopf announced that Iraq's military machine was on the verge of collapse. The Iraqis were losing a hundred tanks a day, he noted, an attrition rate no army can survive. The General did not openly come out and say so, but the clear implication of his statement was that the battlefield was ready for the ground assault. The Air Force and Navy had essentially done their job, it was now up to the Army and Marines to enter Kuwait and mop up the frightened and demoralized Iraqis.

In his briefing, the U.S. commander admitted also what most serious observers of the U.S.-Iraqi military balance had known all along. Iraq's military forces had been no match for the U.S. and U.N. forces assembled in the Gulf. Iraq had no navy and its air force lacked sophisticated air defenses to confront the U.S. and allied air forces. As for its army, after fighting Iran for eight years, the Iraqi soldiers were simply too tired and demoralized to do battle again.

The Iraqi losses in the war, by any measure, were astonishing. Four weeks into the air battle (i.e., as of February 13), most of Iraq's nuclear, biological, and chemical infrastructure had been destroyed, and so had its command and control structure, innumerable airfields, power plants, military installations, and industrial plants. In Kuwait and southern Iraq, site for the next phase of the war, 1,300 tanks, 1,100 artillery pieces, and 800 armored personnel carriers (one-third of the Iraqi tank force and artillery deployed there) had already been destroyed. A week later, by February 20, the losses had risen to 1,700 tanks, 1,450 artillery pieces, and 900 personnel carriers. The Iraqi military forces in Kuwait and southern Iraq were fast reaching the end of their rope.

DEFINING OBJECTIVES

The War Aims Debate Continues

With the Iranian, Iraqi, and Soviet peace overtures scorned, the battlefield softened, and a ground offensive all but imminent, it was only logical for Americans to wonder: Where do we go from here? How far did America's commitment extend in the Gulf? Did it end with the liberation of Kuwait and the restoration to his throne of the Emir, or was America under moral obligation also to destroy the remainder of Iraq's war machine and to remove from power Saddam Hussein himself? The more Americans pondered these questions, the more dubious and ambivalent the answers became.

The legal authority, of course, for America's military presence in the Gulf and the use of force were the twelve U.N. resolutions of 1990 that condemned Iraq's invasion of Kuwait, authorized the economic sanctions, and held Iraq responsible for damages resulting from the war. Presumably, the moment that Iraq was out of Kuwait, the Emir restored to his throne, and the government in Baghdad in compliance with the U.N. resolutions, the U.S. commitment was over.

A great many Americans agreed with this assessment. Short of an unexpected catastrophe, the United States appeared to be exiting the war with a decisive military victory, with the U.N. and congressionally approved war aims fulfilled, with fewer casualties than originally feared, and with its friends and allies in the Arab world pleased with the outcome. Why gamble these gains for goals and objectives whose fulfillment would be far from certain? The U.N. Security Council had not ordered Saddam Hussein's removal from power or the destruction of his war machine, only the withdrawal of his forces from Kuwait. Expanding on the dictates of the United Nations by attempting also to force Saddam out of power could well require a military campaign deep into Iraq--a venture high in casualties and political risks for the region. Making Saddam the target of America could consecrate the Iraqi leader as a martyr in the eyes of the Arab world and turn his military defeat into political victory. It made even less sense to want to attack Iraq's remaining military forces--those not involved in the occupation of Kuwait. With Syria, Iran, and the Kurds lingering at the sidelines eager for the opportunity to devour major parts of Iraqi territory, it was not difficult to perceive why a militarily wasted Iraq was not in the U.S. national interest.

Many more Americans, however, disagreed with this assessment.[7] This is no time, they argued, for face-saving diplomatic formulas designed to spare Saddam Hussein. The United States, having challenged the Iraqi leader, must now assume responsibility for the successful conclusion of the war and for the peace that must follow. Peace and stability in the Middle East can only come in the context of a conclusive U.S. military victory, one that will destroy Saddam's war machine and remove from power the Iraqi leader himself. Allowing Iraq to exit the war with a share of its military forces intact and Saddam Hussein still in power would only lead to greater postwar traumas. The war would have served no purpose if after weeks of fighting the world merely returned to the status quo of August 1, 1990.

Kuwait alone is no longer the issue, they argued. Saddam Hussein is one of the main reasons this war is being fought. The Iraqi leader has displayed such cruelty in his dealings with his own people and toward his neighbors that he deserves to be removed from office, his regime and war machine to be destroyed. A new leadership must be installed in Iraq, one devoid of territorial ambitions and committed to live in peace with its neighbors. Mortimer B. Zuckerman, editor-in-chief of *U.S. News and World Report*, perceptively summarized the viewpoint of the expanded war zealots when he wrote, "The problems of the Middle East will not disappear with Saddam, but they are insoluble as long as he remains in power."[8]

The Search for a "Secure and Peaceful" Middle East

While Americans at home were debating war aims and how far the war should go, a far more pivotal debate was taking place in the corridors of the United Nations and in the foreign policy establishments of the coalition nations. At stake was the shape of the postwar Middle East, now that victory was near, and the arrangements that were required if peace and security were ever to prevail in the troubled region.

Many members of the coalition had their own plans for a postwar peace, but surprisingly, the United States was not one of them. Six months into the crisis, five weeks into the war, Washington still had no clear plans for a postwar Middle East. The United States had "thoughts" on the matter, it had "ideas," but nothing of the kind that could result in a Middle East better than the one that Saddam Hussein had tried to violate. Admirers of America, even critics, wondered: Had not the defeat of Iraqi aggression and America's victory in the war improved prospects for a more secure Middle East?

The first hint of where America stood on the issue was given by Secretary of State James Baker in February 1991. The United States, he noted in testimony before a congressional committee, would strive for a postwar settlement that addressed the region's most critical needs, that is, regional security, arms control, the reduction of economic disparities, and settlement of the Arab-Israeli conflict. The United States was prepared to help the region solve these problems, but would impose no solutions--repeat: impose no solutions. The Secretary's message undoubtedly pleased some audiences (especially the nations of the region that favored a "hands-off" U.S. postwar policy), but it certainly disappointed many others.

No one, of course, had expected the Secretary to announce a postwar Pax Americana. Modern history had adequately demonstrated that no single nation could impose its will on the Middle East or remake the region in its own image, and the United States was no exception. The future peace and security of the Gulf was for the nations of the region to determine, but America had to provide appropriate leadership, such as it did when it organized an international coalition to confront Saddam Hussein. The Secretary's statement offered no such leadership, other than for a vague promise of help in solving the area's "critical needs." These needs, incidentally, were the very ones that had driven, unsuccessfully, U.S. foreign policy on the Middle East for the past forty years. What the United States-- the world's only superpower--was in effect proposing was to stand by while some of the world's most insurmountable problems, such as the senseless accumulation of weapons of mass destruction in the Middle East and the Arab-Israeli conflict, were tackled by someone else.

On the subject of regional security, for instance, the United States was offering nothing more than the status quo--no future military presence, no peacekeeping forces, only the continuation of the long-standing U.S. naval presence in the region. Granted that the basic responsibility for the security of the Gulf should remain with the nations of the region, who but the United States could maintain the delicate balance of power needed to keep the area's five chief antagonists--Israel, Syria, Egypt, Iraq, and Iran--from reaching again at each other's throats? On the Arab-Israeli conflict, too, the Middle East's mega-issue and the one that will ultimately determine the future course of events in the region, the United States was not playing. The war had created new opportunities, noted Secretary Baker, and the United States was prepared to assist in the process of reconciliation between Arabs and Israelis, as well as in the resolution of the Palestinian problem. Secretaries of State going back to the days of President Eisenhower have used identical language, but to no avail. There was a notable change, though, in the U.S. policy on the region and one that the Secretary mentioned only peripherally. Future initiatives toward an Arab-Israeli peace and regional security in the Gulf would heavily involve the Soviet Union also. Acknowledging the Soviets as an active Middle East player was the price Washington had to pay for the Soviet Union's reluctant membership in the U.N. coalition against Iraq.

February 22, 1991

THE PRESIDENT'S ULTIMATUM

The President's ultimatum was issued on February 22 (see Appendix I). It demanded the start of "large-scale" withdrawal of Saddam's forces from Kuwait, beginning at noon EST on Saturday, February 23 or the consequences would be an allied ground attack. The entire withdrawal, said the ultimatum, should be completed within one week, with Kuwait City to be freed within the first forty-eight hours.

The ultimatum, it will be recalled, was issued while the Iraqi Foreign Minister was still in Moscow agreeing to some loose ends on Gorbachev's peace plan. Iraq had already assented to withdraw from Kuwait and to release the U.S. and allied prisoners of war it was holding. Two major differences still remained. Under the Soviet plan, the Iraqi withdrawal from Kuwait would be completed within three weeks and be followed by the lifting of all U.N. resolutions covering sanctions, reparations, and arms sales against Iraq. Under the terms of the U.S. ultimatum, Iraq would have to evacuate Kuwait within one week (and thus leave behind much of its heavy equipment), and all resolutions against it would remain in effect until lifted by the U.N. Security Council.

The differences between the two plans were by no means insurmountable and could have been reconciled with a minimum of diplomacy. Iraq was in no position to bargain and most certainly would have agreed to the President's one-week withdrawal timetable at the first indication of joint U.S.- Soviet pressure. As for the future of the U.N. anti-Iraqi resolutions, the United States, by virtue of its veto power in the U.N. Security Council, had the power to insist on their continuation for as long as it wanted to. But the President was in no mood to either "negotiate" or allow the Soviet Union to control the war's end game. He wanted to bring Saddam Hussein to his knees and to do it without Soviet help, even at the expense of a potentially bloody ground war. A graceful Iraqi exit from Kuwait (which would have been the result of the Soviet initiative) was definitely not on the President's agenda.

In many ways, what the President's ultimatum did not say was as important as what it did say. By insisting that the Iraqi forces leave Kuwait within one week and that the U.N. resolutions against Iraq remain in effect, the President was clearly signaling his intention to punish Iraq but not destroy it. The removal of the Iraqi forces from Kuwait, the restoration of the Emir to his throne, and Iraq's compliance with the U.N. resolutions were the only U.S. war aims; not, as some had been demanding, the liquidation of Saddam's regime, the allied control of his country, and destruction of his entire war machine.

The debate over war aims once again became academic at noon of February 23 EST, when Saddam Hussein in one of his greatest blunders of the war simply ignored the President's ultimatum, which would have allowed his army an unmolested exit from Kuwait and spared the lives of thousands. Was the Iraqi leader's refusal to comply with the President's ultimatum a gross policy miscalculation, or had Moscow possibly assured the Iraqi of its ability to shelter him from the impending doom? A few hours after the lapse of the President's deadline, Saddam through his Foreign Minister in Moscow did agree to the immediate and unconditional withdrawal of its forces from Kuwait; forty-eight hours later he even signed off on an order to the troops themselves to begin withdrawing. Why then Saddam's decision to ignore the President's ultimatum? Future historians will ponder this question, as they will undoubtedly reflect on the rationale for the President's very generous terms to Iraq in his February 22 ultimatum. Had Saddam Hussein accepted these terms, the President's open resolve to humiliate Iraq militarily would have eluded him.

NOTES

1. *Washington Post*, February 16, 1991.

2. Yevgeni Primakov, "My Final Visit with Saddam Hussein," *Time*, March 11, 1991.

3. Thomas L. Friedman, "Soviet Initiative: Is Half a Loaf Enough for Bush?", *New York Times*, February 20, 1991.

4. Yevgeni Primakov, "My Final Visit with Saddam Hussein," *Time*, March 11, 1991.

5. Michael Dobbs and Rick Atkinson, "Soviets Say Iraq's Response Positive; Bush Calls Pullout Plan Unacceptable," *Washington Post*, February 22, 1991.

6. Charles Krauthammer, "The Ground War: Hold It Off," *Washington Post*, February 10, 1991.

7. In a *Washington Post*/ABC News Poll conducted on February 22, 1991, 71 percent of those questioned expressed the view that the final objective of the war with Iraq should be "to force Saddam Hussein out of power." Only 28 percent believed that the goal should be to drive the Iraqis out of Kuwait.

8. Mortimer B. Zuckerman, "The Real Issue of the Gulf War," *U.S. News and World Report*, February 18, 1991.

4 The Hundred-Hour Ground War

Any hope that the Gulf region would somehow be spared the ordeal of a ground war faded at noon (EST) on Saturday, February 23, when Saddam Hussein, for reasons known only to himself, ignored the fairly generous terms of the President's ultimatum, electing instead to throw his lot with the uncertainties of the Soviet peace initiative. There is no evidence that Iraq intends to comply with the U.S. terms, declared the White House within minutes of the lapse of the U.S. deadline; neither has the United Nations received a communication from Baghdad to this effect. The U.S. announcement proceeded to thank President Gorbachev "for his extensive efforts," but noted that his proposal was "unacceptable" because it did not provide for an unequivocal Iraqi commitment to withdraw from Kuwait immediately and unconditionally. Iraq's approval of the Soviet peace plan, therefore, was without effect.

Closing the door to the Soviet initiative, gently but firmly, freed the President for the final stage of his showdown with Iraq--the destruction of Saddam Hussein's weary army in Kuwait. He had made the decision to launch a ground offensive weeks ago;[1] all that remained now was the official announcement. "I have directed General Norman Schwarzkopf," the President told waiting reporters in the White House press room later that evening, "to use all forces available under his command, *including ground forces*, to eject the Iraqi army from Kuwait." The ground war, long feared by millions, was under way.

GENERAL SCHWARZKOPF AND HIS "HAIL MARY"

It was hardly a contest. The world's best-trained and best-equipped troops, employing superior strategy and tactics, and enjoying complete air superiority over the battlefield, confronted on the sands of Kuwait an Iraqi army tired of war, short of food and water, and exhausted from the gruesome air and sea bombardment of the past five weeks. The fearsome troops, the lethal armor, the artillery and chemical weapons, the ferocious fortifications that Saddam Hussein had threatened the coalition with were nowhere to be seen. What the U.S. and allied ground troops encountered in the morning hours of February 24 was truly a "paper tiger," an army totally devoid of the will and capability to fight and with only two viable options: surrender or die.

The destitute shape of the Iraqi army surprised even the most ardent supporters of the ground war. Had the army that Saddam Hussein deployed in Kuwait and with which he had hoped to devastate the "infidels" in the "mother of all battles" truly been a paper tiger? Was U.S. intelligence so badly deceived in its estimates of the military worth of the Iraqi troops? Were all the gloomy predictions of savage hand-to-hand fighting, of Iraqi brutality, and of the thousands of body bags been nothing more than journalistic speculation?

No! Saddam's army, the one that had invaded Kuwait on August 2, 1990, and had aroused the President's ire, had not been a paper tiger. It was a large, well-trained, and combat-tested force equipped with some of the best Soviet, French, and Chinese weapons that oil money could buy. But the Iraqi army that confronted the allies on February 23, 1991, had been badly mauled by the five-week air offensive. And it had also fallen victim to one of the most foolish decisions made by Saddam Hussein during the course of the war--the decision to confront the allies by means of a "static defense strategy."

The air offensive literally devastated the Iraqi army's ability to operate as a coherent military force. Not only because of the enormous casualties in men and armor[2] that the allied pilots inflicted on the dug-in Iraqis; equally fatal was the chaos on the battlefield that resulted from the devastation of the Iraqi army's command and control systems. Deprived of even the most rudimentary communications and without real-time intelligence on the enemy and his movements, the organizational discipline and command authority of Saddam's army quickly disintegrated. Whatever plans the Iraqi high command might have had for putting up an organized resistance against the allies or for counterattacking evaporated quickly when Iraqi field commanders were unable to communicate with each other and with their troops. With the allied forces in southern Iraq executing a sweeping maneuver and cutting off the northern Iraqi routes of escape, and with thousands of allied vehicles penetrating the Iraqi defenses along the Kuwaiti-Iraqi border, the totally shocked and disorganized Iraqis fell back in retreat or just surrendered. Less than forty-eight hours after the start of the allied offensive, long before the planned assault was to reach its full climax, Saddam's army collapsed. Never before in history had an army been made more impotent or been more thoroughly devastated from the air.

The "static defense strategy"--Saddam's strategy for hanging on to the prize of his aggression--similarly contributed to the swift collapse of his army. Half a million men were used to implement this strategy, deployed in an intricate three-tier defensive system.[3] The first defensive tier, consisting of elaborate fortifications, dug-in armor, and mine fields, was designed to stop the advancing allied forces and to expose them to intense Iraqi artillery fire. Allied troops that succeeded in penetrating the first-tier defenses would then be confronted by the second tier, a large mechanized force held in reserve in the vicinity of Kuwait City. A third defensive tier of Republican Guard troops, Saddam's best-trained and best-equipped soldiers, deployed in a crescent pattern north of the Iraqi-Kuwait border, would then counterattack and destroy whatever forces had penetrated the previous two tiers.

The "static defense strategy" was reminiscent of the one used by Saddam Hussein successfully in his eight-year war against Iran. What the strategy failed to provide for, however, were the very important U.S. strengths in the areas of air power and armor (which the Iranians did not have), especially the ability of the U.S. mechanized forces to conduct sweeping flanking movements around and past the Iraqi defenses. So unyielding was the Iraqi leader in his application of this strategy and in his determination to hold on to Kuwait that he failed to extend his first tier line of fortifications much beyond the 160-mile-long Iraqi-Kuwait border. This unprotected left flank, as we shall see later, caused the Iraqi army's ultimate doom.

10 p.m. EST February 23,
to 10 p.m. EST February 25, 1991

The Strategy behind Desert Storm:
The First Forty-Eight Hours

Listening to General Schwarzkopf tell it, as he did in his now-famous briefing to the media on the afternoon of February 27, when he first began contemplating the use of force to evict the Iraqis from Kuwait, he was confronted with some pretty bad odds. The Iraqis outnumbered him 3 to 2 on overall troop strengths, 2 to 1 in the number of combat troops.[4] In addition they had 4,700 tanks versus his and the allies' 3,500, and a great deal more artillery. To attack a position, the General reminded his audience, one needs a troop ratio of 3 to 1 (5 to 1 if the position is heavily fortified), and before the air campaign he did not have these ratios.

The air campaign, of course, made up the difference. Bombing raids by allied pilots devastated the defensive posture of the Iraqi forces, especially of the troops deployed along the frontal line barrier, Iraq's first defensive tier. The air campaign also took out all bridges and supply lines leading south, effectively blocking reinforcements and supplies from entering the theater of operations. When all of Iraq's forty-odd divisions in Kuwait and southern Iraq had been hurt, when the front-line divisions had been attrited to 50 percent of their strength, General Schwarzkopf was ready to strike.

He actually struck in two areas: along the Saudi-Kuwaiti border in the south, where Saddam Hussein had expected him to, and also in the west, in an area along the Saudi-Iraqi border where an earlier U.S. deception had caused the Iraqis to leave a gaping hole, devoid of troops or armor. To the surprise of almost all "war gurus," however, the American commander did not send the Marines ashore in Kuwait. The amphibious landing that had been rumored for months, as the surest way for freeing Kuwait City without having to confront the Iraqi defenses in the south, actually proved to be a deception. It worked beautifully and tied up six Iraqi divisions against an amphibious landing that never came. Since they had arrived in the Gulf the American Marines had conspicuously and repeatedly practiced amphibious landings and, as zero hour approached, an armada of thirty-one ships headed by the USS *Nassau* swung into position as if ready to come ashore. The battleships *Missouri* and *Wisconsin* took turns firing their guns. It was all a feint. The war ended with the U.S. Marines still aboard their landing craft.   Along the Saudi-Kuwaiti border, however, Saddam's first tier of defense, the Marines once again proved their superior weapons and training. Supported by Saudi, Egyptian, and Kuwaiti forces, the 1st and 2nd U.S. Marine divisions crossed the Iraqi bunkers and other fortifications "like it was water" (the description is General Schwarzkopf's) and charged in the direction of Kuwait City. The dug-in Iraqis hardly even put up a fight. Lacking air support and exhausted from the allied aerial bombardment of the previous five weeks, they surrendered first in squads, then in entire platoons. Less than forty-eight hours after the President had given the order to attack, the U.S. Marines were poised to enter Kuwait City.

But it was in the west that the disabling of Iraq's large and modern air forces paid the biggest dividends. With the Iraqi commanders deprived of their eyes and ears on the battlefield, General Schwarzkopf directed, about ten days before the start of the campaign, a massive movement of troops and materiel to a huge assembly area west of the Wadi al Batin, the dry river bed that separates Kuwait from Iraq. Amazingly, the massive move totally escaped the Iraqis' attention. By the time the President's attack order was given, 150,000 men, at least 1,200 tanks, and hundreds of thousands of tons of water, food, fuel, ammunition, and spare parts were in place and ready to go. The staging area, noted General Schwarzkopf, held enough supplies to last him sixty days, just in case "we got into a slugfest battle, which we easily could have gotten into."

In the morning hours of February 24, Baghdad time, an enormous force of U.S., British, and French forces--a total of ten divisions--crossed the Saudi-Iraqi border. Attacking furthest west, about two hundred miles from where the Marines were fighting in Kuwait, was the French 6th Armored Division and the 82nd U.S. Airborne Division. They were the "flank" troops, whose mission was to protect the main invading force on their right from any Iraqi surprises originating in the northwest. (They never did.) Paralleling the "flank" troops were five columns of armor-rich units, General Schwarzkopf's "Hail Mary" receivers, consisting from west to east of the 101st Airborne Division, the 24th Mechanized Infantry Division, the 1st and 3rd Armored Divisions, the 1st Infantry Division, the 1st Cavalry

Division, and the 1st British Armored Division. Two of the columns charged straight ahead in the direction of the Euphrates River, to secure the River and to block the Iraqi routes of escape. This part of the mission accomplished, they were then to turn east and confront the Iraqi Republican Guard divisions dug in along the Iraqi-Kuwait border. The remaining three columns similarly charged north, but quickly swung east to join the allied forces attacking Kuwait City. The entire flanking maneuver worked like a charm and encountered only scant opposition. Less than forty-eight hours after the ground offensive had begun, all preliminary moves had been completed, the Iraqi routes of escape north had been severed, and the allies were within striking distance of the Republican Guards, the last remaining Iraqi forces able to put up a fight.

6 p.m. EST, February 25, 1991

Saddam's Withdrawal Order

The President's attack order, it will be recalled, was issued at 10 p.m. (EST), Saturday, February 23. Less than forty-eight hours later Saddam Hussein was ready to throw in the towel. "In the name of God, the merciful, the compassionate," read the statement on Baghdad radio in the morning hours of Tuesday, February 26 (6 p.m. EST, Monday, February 25).

Our armed forces have performed their holy duty. . . . They have been engaged in an epic, valiant battle that will be recorded by history in letters of light. The leadership has stressed its acceptance to withdraw in accordance with U.N. Council Resolution 660 when it agreed to the Soviet peace proposal. On this basis, and in compliance with this decision, orders were issued to the armed forces for an organized withdrawal to the positions in which they were before the 1st of August 1990. This is regarded as a practical compliance with Resolution 660.

The statement was not entirely unexpected. With General Schwarzkopf's armor columns already poised in southern Iraq, with Kuwait City within reach of the allies, and with thousands of Iraqi soldiers surrendering to the advancing Americans, Saddam's Kuwait adventure was quickly coming to an end.

To be sure, the statement from Baghdad addressed only the Iraqi withdrawal from Kuwait, not the return of the allied POWs or Iraq's readiness to comply with the remaining U.N. resolutions, both key U.S. demands before a cease-fire could take effect. Had the United States wished to end at that point the killing of the helpless and demoralized Iraqis, it could have easily challenged Baghdad on the missing issues. With its military forces in total disarray and allied armor in control of the principal escape routes north, Iraq was in no position to bargain. It would have readily acceded to any U.S. terms for ending the war, had the United States only asked.

But the United States elected not to ask. We will continue to prosecute the war, noted Marlin Fitzwater, the White House press secretary, on learning of the Iraqi withdrawal order. We have heard of no reason to change that, and because there is a war on, our first concern must be the safety and security of U.S. and coalition troops.

"Saddam's most recent speech is an outrage," proclaimed President Bush angrily the following morning. "He is not withdrawing; his defeated forces are retreating and he is trying to claim victory in the midst of a rout." The implication of the President's statement was clear: with the ground war going America's way and the Iraqi army overwhelmed on all fronts, it made no difference whether Iraq wanted the fighting to end or not. The United States, which was holding all the cards, was determined to go on with the war, and Iraq had better abandon any hope for an "organized withdrawal." The opportunity for a graceful exit from Kuwait had passed at noon on February 23, the date that Iraq ignored the President's ultimatum. Once the ground war had started, it could only end by an Iraqi unconditional "surrender" or by the total defeat of Saddam's army at the hands of General Schwarzkopf.

By insisting, however, that the Iraqis were *retreating* and not *withdrawing*, the President inadvertently added a troublesome issue to the moral dimension of the conflict. "We will not attack unarmed soldiers in retreat," he declared, "but we have no choice but to consider retreating combat units as a threat and respond accordingly." Note that the President said *retreating* combat units, not *withdrawing* combat units, meaning that Iraqi units withdrawing from Kuwait (under orders from Baghdad) would not be safe from air attacks or the pursuit by allied ground forces. The distinction puzzled many Americans. Was this a case of hairsplitting to justify the continuation

of the war, the crushing of Iraq's war machine, and the public
humiliation of Saddam? Of what possible military value was the
continued killing of Saddam's demoralized and beaten troops,
regardless of whether they were "retreating" or "withdrawing"?[5]

Technically, the President was not obliged to comply with the Iraqi
leader's order for "an organized withdrawal." (It would have been
different, of course, had Saddam ordered his troops to "surrender,"
since under international law a surrender order requires all fighting
to stop.) Granted that Saddam did not order his troops to "surrender"
but only to "withdraw"; granted, too, that the rules of war allowed the
United States and its allies to attack retreating or withdrawing troops
until they had surrendered; did this refusal by Saddam, whom we
knew to be cruel and indifferent to the loss of human life and whom
we had repeatedly compared to Hitler, justify the brutal slaughter of
the retreating Iraqis during the final days of the war, while they were
trying desperately to leave Kuwait? At home, few persons appeared
troubled by the legalism of this senseless killing. Americans who
instinctively protest "blows below the belt" or who condemn "hitting
someone when he is down" took it all in stride. It was all part of war,
they reasoned; a price Iraq had to pay for confronting the United
States.

At the U.N. Security Council, too, few voices were raised in
support of Saddam's withdrawal offer or in favor of stopping the war.
Cuba and Yemen, as expected, came in strong on the side of Iraq and
demanded an unconditional halt to all fighting, but their voices were
soon eclipsed by the unity of the U.N. coalition. As for the Soviet
Union, it wavered badly throughout the debate, uncertain of the
direction it should follow. It obviously liked the respectability that
membership in the U.N. coalition brought it, but it was also becoming
increasingly weary with the U.S. President's apparent insistence on
waging war until Saddam Hussein had been thoroughly defeated and
discredited. The Iraqi leader has raised the white flag of surrender,
pleaded the Soviet spokesman at the Council. He can be trusted to
withdraw from Kuwait. But after espousing Iraq's cause for several
days, on February 26 the Soviet Union finally decided to side with the
other members of the U.N. coalition in demanding that Saddam
accept *all* U.N. Security Council resolutions before the fighting could
stop. Perhaps Baghdad's unpredictable behavior throughout the
period of the Soviet peace initiative convinced Moscow that

continuing to promote Saddam Hussein before the international community was the surest way to lose friends and respect.

10 p.m. EST, February 25, to
midnight EST, February 27, 1991

The Rout--Destroying a Beaten Army

Saddam's "organized withdrawal" from Kuwait began as scheduled during the night of February 25. Thousands of vehicles of all types-- tanks, armored personnel carriers, trucks, tractor-trailers, fuel tankers, ambulances, buses, private cars--began the trek north on the only available good highway leading to Iraq, the six-lane road linking Kuwait City with Basra, via Mutlaa and Safwan. Before long, the sheer number of vehicles caused traffic to stall, so the fleeing Iraqis opened a second evacuation route, this one along the coast via Subiya and Umm Qasr.

The withdrawal remained "organized" for probably no longer than an hour. In one of the most ferocious and savage episodes of the war, Saddam's hope for an "organized withdrawal" was transformed-- courtesy of the U.S. Air Force, Navy, and Marines--into a cruel and morally unjustified massacre of thousands of fleeing men. The war, which had been launched for the purpose of forcing Iraq's troops out of Kuwait, was ending with the Iraqis desperately trying to leave the emirate and the U.S. forces holding them back and killing them.

The Iraqis had hardly come out of their dug-in positions, their convoys had barely been formed, when wave after wave of U.S. Air Force, Navy, and Marine close-air support aircraft took up the attack against them. Those in the front and rear were struck first, trapping in the middle hundreds of vehicles. Unable to move or even take shelter from the incessant air attacks, the panicked Iraqis drove into the desert only to become bogged down there, too, by soft sand and land mines that they themselves had planted. Scores of vehicles were blown apart, burned, or shattered in the allied attacks, their occupants killed instantly. By morning, despite the mangled scenes of destruction and death along both highways and in the surrounding desert, the allied aircraft returned, attacking the convoys again and again with cluster bombs or whatever other munitions were readily available to aircraft crews. Pilots returning from their raids described gruesome scenes of devastation and carnage, with the retreating Iraqis desperately trying to evade and the attacking U.S. aircraft picking them off one after another. It was like "shooting fish in a barrel," declared one U.S. pilot; "the biggest Fourth of July show ever," noted another; "it looks like the road to Daytona Beach in spring break," said a third. So many aircraft were attacking the helpless Iraqis that allied air controllers worried over the possibility of midair collisions. By the time the last tank and vehicle had been destroyed, the entire area north of Kuwait City was a tangled sea of scorched, twisted metal littered with bodies of Iraqi soldiers. "The carnage and destruction," reported two respected war correspondents, "resembled a great martial demolition derby."[6]

While the one-sided slaughter of the retreating Iraqis continued, military spokesmen in Riyadh and Washington attempted to rationalize the savage and appalling attack. The Iraqis, said the U.S. Command briefer in Riyadh, were not withdrawing from Kuwait, but were being pushed away from the battlefield! The United States had no assurance that the Iraqi troops were really going home; their movements could be for the purpose of reinforcing the Republican Guards still fighting along the Iraqi-Kuwait border. The command had an obligation to protect its forces on the battlefield, the official spokesmen noted, and to cut off potential reinforcements to units still engaged in combat against the allies. If the Iraqis fleeing Kuwait wanted to avoid allied firepower, they should abandon their weapons and armor and come out in the open. Until such time, U.S. aircraft would continue to pursue and destroy them.

These explanations notwithstanding, many at home and abroad agonized over the awesome carnage. How could the demoralized and beaten Iraqi soldiers fleeing Kuwait pose a threat to the allies? Without armor and lacking air support, the Iraqi forces of February 25 and 26 packed less punch than the frail Kuwaiti army that had faced them on August 2, 1990. The killing of the thousands of fleeing Iraqis from Kuwait was devoid of any military necessity. It was a political act of vengeance, pure and simple, that had nothing to do with the legal authority for the war. The U.N. Security Council had authorized the use of force to compel Iraq's withdrawal from Kuwait to the positions it occupied on August 1, 1990, not the destruction of its fleeing army.

Midnight EST, February 27, 1991

The Interim Cease-Fire

Despite the thousands of men left behind in Kuwait, the end for the Iraqi army did not really come until the morning hours of February 27, when U.S. and British armored forces attacked and destroyed most of what was left of the Republican Guard divisions southwest of Basra. With units of the U.S. 101st Airborne and 24th Mechanized Divisions poised on the banks of the Euphrates River and along Highway 8 (the principal Iraqi escape routes north), with all Euphrates and Tigris river crossings destroyed and under the watchful eye of the allies, and with the entire area southwest of Basra under the control of U.S. and British armored columns, the "gate" on Saddam's forces in Kuwait finally closed. (The closing of the gate more than any other U.S. action, proved that the purpose of the U.S. offensive was to destroy the Iraqi army, not merely to force it to withdraw. Had the United States wished only to force the Iraqis out of Kuwait, it would have allowed an escape route for their use.)

"Kuwait is liberated, Iraq's army is defeated, and our military objectives have been met," announced President Bush in a special address to the nation at 9 p.m. EST on February 27. "After consulting with Secretary of Defense Cheney, the Chairman of the Joint Chiefs of Staff, General Powell, and our coalition partners, I am pleased to announce that at midnight tonight EST, exactly 100 hours since ground operations commenced, and six weeks since the start of Operation Desert Storm, all U.S. and coalition forces will suspend offensive combat operations." The President then proceeded to spell out what he said were the terms with which Iraq had to comply under the terms of the cease-fire: the release of all allied POWs and Kuwaiti detainees, information on the location of land and sea mines, and Iraq's unconditional pledge to comply fully with all relevant U.N. resolutions.

The President's order caused all organized fighting to stop almost immediately, except for sporadic shooting by isolated small Iraqi units that somehow never heard the news. An eerie stillness returned to the battlefield, littered with the debris of the violent battle of the previous days. Before too long, Iraqi soldiers by the thousands--many barefoot boys and malnourished older men--emerged from their hiding places to resume the trek back home or to simply surrender to the allied authorities.

Four days later, in the Iraqi city of Safwan, General Schwarzkopf, accompanied by several senior allied commanders, accepted what for all practical purposes was Iraq's surrender on the battlefield. It was all a formality. On the evening of February 28, three days earlier, Tariq Aziz, Deputy Prime Minister and Foreign Minister of Iraq, had already agreed on behalf of Iraq to comply with Security Council Resolution 660 and all other pertinent resolutions.

Did the President End the War Prematurely?

Few of the President's decisions relating to the Gulf war are as controversial as his order that ended hostilities on February 27. With the "gate" closed, the encirclement of the helpless Iraqis complete, was the President's decision ending the war a humane and courageous act designed to spare the loss of additional human life (admittedly Iraqi life), or was it a blunder that allowed thousands of Saddam's troops to escape? The issue may have been only of academic interest here, but it had a real life-and-death significance to the millions of Shiites in southern Iraq, who in the aftermath of the war had foolishly taken up arms against Saddam Hussein only to find themselves confronted and crushed by the Republican Guards and other Iraqi troops escaping from Kuwait because of the President's order.

The controversy over the President's decision exploded into a major policy squabble late in March 1991, when General Schwarzkopf in a nationally televised interview volunteered the information that, had it not been for the President's order, "we could have completely closed the door and made it, in fact, a battle of annihilation."[7] The clear implication of the statement was that the allied forces could have finished Saddam's regime but were denied the opportunity by the President's order. Within a couple of days, however, especially after the Secretary of Defense reminded General Schwarzkopf that he had not raised any objections to terminating the hostilities on February 27 when he had been contacted, the General, a loyal and committed soldier, recanted his statement. He was extremely sorry, he told reporters, that a poor choice of words would result in dishonor cast upon the President.

General Schwarzkopf's apology may have ended his disastrous spat with the President but it did not settle the underlying question: Was the President wrong in ordering the cease-fire when he did?[8] The answer depends on one's perspective. Given more time, of course, the allies could have killed more Iraqis[9] and deprived Saddam of some of the troops and armor that he used later to crush the Shiite rebellion. But continuing the war past the point of the Iraqis' total defeat would have raised serious questions about America's moral fiber and leadership qualities. The allies' goal in the war was to force Saddam Hussein out of Kuwait; the U.S. goal additionally was to destroy his offensive military capabilities; and both goals had been achieved long before the President declared the cease-fire.

THE MOST POPULAR WAR EVER

Destroying the Vietnam Syndrome

Until February 1991, most Americans had never experienced the national high that comes from "winning" a war. The United States had won World War II, but that was back in 1945 before 70 percent of all Americans living today were born. The war that most Americans remember and have lived through was Vietnam, the military and political fiasco of the late 1960s and early 1970s, which ended with terrified American diplomats, GIs, and their allies at the rooftop of the Saigon Embassy, struggling to escape the approaching victorious North Vietnamese.

The Vietnam disaster left Americans deeply divided and uncertain of their role in the world. When the U.S.-led forces late in February crushed Iraq, they also crushed the divisions and uncertainties of the Vietnam era. The Gulf war did nothing, of course, to correct America's problems at home (poverty and homelessness, unemployment and unequal health care of its citizens), but it did sweep away in one giant surge of exhilaration and optimism all the doubts Americans had felt over their role in the world and the limits of their power. The nation suddenly felt united under a President with a clear vision and a willingness to use force. Instead of American GIs running scared as they did atop the Embassy in Saigon, they were now returning home victors; instead of being damned and ridiculed, they were being welcomed as allies and liberators. This war, like World War II, was ending with flags flying high and with the troops held in esteem, not in shame and doubt as was the case after Vietnam. Expectations of American leadership in the world once again flourished. President Bush contributed much toward these feelings of euphoria when he declared, on March 1, 1991, "By God, we've kicked the Vietnam syndrome once and for all," and by his address to the Congress (see Appendix J) a few days later, when he spoke glowingly and optimistically of America's hopes for resolving the many challenges in the aftermath of the liberation of Kuwait.

Much of the success for destroying the Vietnam syndrome rests of course with President Bush, who took special care to ensure that the mistakes of Vietnam would not be repeated. The Vietnam war, it will be recalled, was essentially a U.S. operation, with little if any support from the international community (but with plenty of criticism and condemnation). This time around, the U.S. involvement was part of an international coalition, clean and unencumbered. In the Vietnam war, unproven strategies of "escalation" and "limited war" determined the scope and level of fighting and were responsible more than anything else for the U.S. military's inability to finish the job. In Kuwait, however, President Bush did not go into the offensive until he had on hand a massive force, and then some, equipped with the best weapons in America's arsenal. During the Vietnam war, President Johnson tried to work with the Congress every step of the way, only to find himself totally frustrated by the great number and variety of dissenting voices. President Bush, however, kept the Congress at arm's length throughout the Kuwaiti war planning phase. When the Congress was asked, a few days before the launching of the air offensive, to render an opinion, all it could obviously do (at that late stage) was to acquiesce. One area in which the President's performance was truly remarkable was his success in marshaling U.S. public opinion in support of the war.[10] By portraying Saddam as a bully who had to be stopped, by equating him with Hitler, and by proclaiming that the war to liberate Kuwait was "just and moral" when all evidence pointed otherwise, the President succeeded in totally crushing whatever opposition existed to the war and its basic aims.

To be sure, Americans always close ranks behind their President in times of war or when confronted with a foreign challenge. President Bush's amazing approval rating of 90 percent on the day the ground offensive was launched was a reflection of this national trait and also of his sustained efforts since August 1990 to enlist public support for his anti-Iraq policies. The President's rating exceeded those of all earlier U.S. chief executives since pollsters began asking questions. Gallup polls, for instance, taken during World War II showed an approval rating of 84 percent for President Franklin D. Roosevelt a month after Pearl Harbor and a rating of 87 percent for President Harry S. Truman after Germany's unconditional surrender. Even President John F. Kennedy received an approval rating of 83 percent in May 1961 despite his bungling of the Bay of Pigs invasion.[11]

The euphoria of victory did not silence the voices of reason. Winning a military victory, they warned, over a nation of 17 million with inferior military capabilities and training did not necessarily herald the arrival a new era. If anything, the victory over Iraq, in the aftermath of equally painless military victories over Grenada, Libya, and the National Guard of Panama, could induce feelings of national arrogance and a bully-boy behavior in American foreign policy. Next time trouble is brewing anywhere in the world, the United States is likely to reach for its guns, before diplomacy or international dialogue are given a chance to resolve the dispute. Rather than gloat over superior military power, yellow ribbons, and ticker tape parades, America should focus on solving its many problems at home and on tidying up its moral behavior.

Lessons Learned

In the aftermath of the war there were lessons learned, but, sadly, many more lessons that were simply being ignored. A nation buoyed by victory on the battlefield and by its sons returning home as heroes was in no mood to hear of mistakes made or of the thousands who lost their lives, not while the ghosts of Vietnam were being laid to rest.

To the vast majority of Americans, Operation Desert Storm was an incredible military victory and one in which the use of *massive and overwhelming military power* triumphed. Desert Storm, noted its admirers, taught America the importance of national resolve and of the proper use of military power, two critical attributes that had been lacking in the Vietnam war. America, they asserted, should heed this lesson: if military power must be used again, it should be massive and overwhelming. Never mind that Hitler's Germany, too, used massive and overwhelming military power against its enemies, or that the United States was unlikely to face any day soon another adversary as dispirited, war-weary, and foolish as Saddam Hussein was. These facts notwithstanding, the use of overwhelming military power to advance national objectives was *the one* and *only* lesson that millions of Americans gained from the war!

There were, of course, several real lessons from the war: some diplomatic; others political, military, and moral. (The use of massive military power to confront a fourth-rate military power was definitely not one of them, since the use of such enormous force against a powerless adversary is a moral issue, not a military one.) Of the politico-military lessons, four stand out.

1. Orchestrating Domestic Support. A flawless, nationwide public relations campaign orchestrated by the White House and supported by a tight control of the news from the Gulf gave the President overwhelming national support for his anti-Iraq policies. It is extremely unlikely that the President would have been able to organize and sustain the international coalition against Saddam Hussein were it not for the strong support that his policies enjoyed at home and with the troops at the front. Despite the President's persistent emphasis on the use of arms over diplomacy during the entire Gulf episode, despite the many cases of outright news management and manipulation, he does deserve a high rating on this one. Had the President failed to garnish popular support for his anti-Iraq policies, the U.S. troops would still be fighting in the Gulf, with Saddam Hussein the certain victor.

2. Defining the Objective. The President rates high marks on this one, also. From day one of the invasion of Kuwait, there was never any doubt about which specific objectives he was pursuing. Despite ambivalence by millions of Americans and even members of the President's immediate staff, the President himself never wavered in his determination to have Iraq evicted from Kuwait, to destroy its military offensive capability, and to force Saddam Hussein to accept *all* U.N. Security Council resolutions. Without clearly defined objectives, without the President pointing the way, the nation and its troops would be floundering as they did in Vietnam.

3. Assessing the Enemy Threat. The relative ease with which the coalition forces routed the Iraqis supports the suspicion that the Iraqi forces were intentionally overrated by the Bush administration. For weeks before the fighting commenced, U.S. and allied military briefers painted dire pictures of Iraqi defenses, of battle-hardened troops, of hundreds of thousands of mines, and of ditches filled with burning oil. The grossly exaggerated assessments of the Iraqi army were not, of course, due to lack of intelligence. The U.S. military had at its disposal the most sophisticated intelligence collection systems ever, and not much concerning the Iraqis escaped it. The gloomy evaluations were designed to justify the massive military force assembled in the Gulf and to prepare U.S. public opinion in the event something went wrong. The manipulation of the "threat," however, accounted also for billions of dollars in unnecessary expenditures to haul unwanted men and materiel to Saudi Arabia from their bases in Germany and the United States, and for the dislocation and disruption suffered by thousands of U.S. reserve and national guard families.

   4. Civilian versus Military Control of Operations. Throughout the war, administration spokesmen took pride in asserting that the White House was not micromanaging the war effort and that General Schwarzkopf in effect was "calling the shots," subject only to broad policy guidance from the President. The approach presumably was designed to correct the Vietnam War's principal command-and-control problem--President Johnson's insistence that target lists first be cleared with him before attack. No one is privy, of course, to the guidance provided General Schwarzkopf by President Bush. The resulting near-total destruction, however, of Iraq's civilian infrastructure and the long-term catastrophic effects on its health and nutrition caused by the allied bombing (see Appendix K) raise serious doubts about the advisability of allowing field commanders to "call the shots" in future conflicts. War, after all, is too serious a business to be left in the hands of generals.

Congress Votes the Money

   Late in February as the jubilant nation began to sense victory in Kuwait, the U.S. Congress suddenly came alive. For seven long months, while the administration was aggressively preparing for war, the great majority of the members of the House and the Senate were nowhere to be seen, shielding themselves behind the congressional calendar (Congress was officially on recess during much of that time) and refraining from any comment that might be interpreted as questioning the President's judgment in dealing with Saddam. With most members back home proclaiming their undying "support for the troops" (and in the process garnishing votes), the silence on Capitol Hill on the more serious issues of war and peace was deafening. Among the legislators, especially those who had voted against the President in January, none was anxious to be labeled "unpatriotic" for having questioned the need for the war.

The war's "money" issue finally energized the Congress. Appropriating money for the conduct of the war was a politically safe thing to do, and even though no one really knew what the total cost of the war ultimately would be, the Congress gleefully set out to tackle the issue. (After all, what was more important than providing the troops with all the support they needed?) The money issue, however, had a wrinkle to it that eventually affected the congressional debate. At U.S. prodding, a dozen or so U.S. allies had pledged to contribute $53.5 billion toward war expenses, but only $14.9 billion had been deposited to the U.S. Treasury by the war's end.[12]

On the assumption that the allies would soon be forthcoming with their contributions, the President late in February 1991 asked the Congress for $15 billion to pay for the U.S. share of the war. The figure was obtained by assuming a total war cost of between $58 billion and $77 billion--including $7 billion to keep troops in the Persian Gulf after the fighting and $5 billion more to return soldiers and equipment to their home bases in the United States and Europe. Of the total war cost, 20 percent or about $15 billion, would be paid by the United States, the balance by the allies. Few knowledgeable persons, of course, took the administration's overall war estimate seriously. War costs, they noted, including the replacement of inventories, aid to Israel and Turkey, forgiving the debts of key Gulf allies (such as Egypt), and the postwar cleanup could easily double that figure. On March 7, 1991, by a vote of 380 to 19, the House of Representatives voted the money requested by the President but also warned the other nations of the coalition to pay up on their pledges. Congress, it noted, "may consider appropriate action" if these commitments were not fulfilled.

THE HUMAN COSTS OF "VICTORY"

No previous conflict in history has ever resulted in so marked a disproportion of casualties.

A total of 390 Americans lost their lives and another 467 were wounded to free Kuwait. This figure includes the 28 service personnel who died in the Iraqi Scud attack on the U.S. billeting facility in Dahran, 21 GIs who were killed by friendly fire, and dozens of others who were overcome by traffic, land mines, or other accidents while stationed in the Gulf. The figure is amazingly low, it actually is miniscule, when considering that the U.S. military presence in the region was 537,000 personnel, supported by 205,000 coalition troops. U.S. losses of armor, planes, and equipment were similarly low, barely exceeding those we lose in peacetime as part of routine military training missions or in accidents.

As for the Iraqi losses, only an approximate count exists. The Defense Intelligence Agency, the one U.S. agency that should know, states that about 100,000 Iraqi soldiers were killed in the fighting, but this figure may have an error factor of 50 percent or higher.[13] Apparently most Iraqis killed in action were buried hastily by their comrades during the fighting or by Arab coalition soldiers after the war, with little regard for detailed record keeping required by international rules. U.S units claim to have buried no more than 1,000 men, but admit that advancing tank units equipped with plows and bulldozers buried under avalanches of sand unknown numbers of enemy soldiers who refused to surrender.

How many of the 100,000 or so Iraqi war dead were actually killed during the massive slaughter of February 25, 26, and 27 is still a mystery. Probably no fewer than 200,000 soldiers started the trek north on the evening of the 25, when ordered to do so by Saddam Hussein, but relatively few bodies were found on the battlefield alongside the hundreds (perhaps thousands) of destroyed and burned tanks and other military vehicles when the fighting ended. What happened to the thousands of Iraqi soldiers who were attempting to flee Kuwait inside these vehicles? Many undoubtedly abandoned their vehicles, electing to cross the desert on foot. But what about the less fortunate ones? Where are their bodies? Who buried them?[14] Journalists who visited the battlefield after the fighting ended, reported seeing heaps of Iraqi corpses buried in mass graves across the desert, but nothing of the size or dimension to explain 100,000 dead.

The Iraqi civilian toll from the allied air raids and the brief internal revolts that followed the war is equally clouded. Preliminary Iraqi estimates claimed that 7,000 civilians lost their lives during the air campaign. Another 30,000 to 50,000 Iraqis, claim opposition leaders, were killed during the bloody Shiite rebellion in the south and in the suppression of the Kurdish revolt in the north. There is little hard information available on any of these figures.[15]

The U.S. government, which has thousands of satellite photos, prisoner interrogations, and human intelligence reports, is not saying, for fear of publicizing the true dimensions of the carnage. Neither is the government of Saddam Hussein, probably for the same reasons.

A fairly good count exists, though, on Iraq's material losses from the war. According to the U.S. military, the allies destroyed or captured about 4,000 of the 4,230 Iraqi tanks that were in the Kuwaiti theater of operations when the war started, 2,140 of its 3,110 artillery pieces, and 1,856 armored vehicles of a prewar total of 2,870.[16] As a result of these losses, all but two of the forty-four divisions assembled by Saddam Hussein to defend Kuwait were destroyed or rendered unfit for battle. The Iraqi expeditionary force, which at one time may have numbered as many as 600,000 men, was reduced to a rabble. For Iraq, which had already lost about 200,000 men in its eight-year war with Iran, the new casualties in the six weeks of fighting represented an enormous loss.

NOTES

1. Thomas L. Friedman and Patrick E. Tyler, "The Path to War: Bush's Crucial Decisions," *New York Times*, March 3, 1991. See also Ann Devroy and Dan Balz, "From Early On, Bush Committed to Ground Assault," *Washington Post*, February 25, 1991.

2. During the week preceding the start of the ground war the Iraqi army was losing 100 tanks a day. It reportedly lost a total of 1,800 tanks, 1,500 artillery pieces, and 1,000 personnel carriers during the five-week air campaign.

3. Michael R. Gordon, "Iraq's Kuwait Defense: 3-Tier Plan That Collapsed," *New York Times*, February 26, 1991.

4. Subsequent events proved that the ratios cited by General Schwarzkopf were not nearly as bad. But the American commander was using an old military axiom of assuming the enemy to have a far greater strength than he actually did (the "maximum threat" theory).

5. A "withdrawal," according to U.S. military authorities, occurs when a nation pulls its forces back from an area without the pressure of attacking forces. A "retreat" occurs when the pullback is required by the action of attacking forces. In this case, according to the same authorities, the Iraqis were "retreating," not "withdrawing."

6. William Claiborne and Caryle Murphy, "Retreat Down Highway of Doom," *Washington Post*, March 2, 1991. See also Steve Coll and William Branigin, "U.S. Scrambled to Shape View of Highway of Death," *Washington Post*, March 11, 1991.

7. George J. Church, "Schwarzkopf's 100 Hours: Too Few?" *Time*, April 8, 1991.

8. According to a *Washington Post*/ABC telephone poll conducted April 3, 1991, a majority of Americans believe that the United States ended the war too soon (as reported in the *Washington Post* on April 5, 1991).

9. The President was right to end the slaughter when he did, commented the *New York Times* editorially on March 29, 1991.

10. Between August 1990 and February 1991, the President's approval rating for handling the Kuwait crisis increased from 60 percent to over 80 percent. The figures are based on 14 polls conducted nationwide by the *New York Times* and CBS News. Similarly, in a series of *Washington Post*/ABC News polls the President's approval rating increased from 80 percent on the day the air offensive began to 90 percent six weeks later when the ground war started.

11. Michael R. Kagay, "Public Shows Support for Ground War," *New York Times*, February 26, 1991.

12. The figure has since been increased to $39.9 billion in cash payments and $5.4 billion in kind assistance.

13. "How Many Iraqis Died?" *Time*, June 17, 1991.

14. Thomas C. Fox, *Iraq: Military Victory; Moral Defeat* (Kansas City: Sheed and Ward, 1991), p. 157.

15. Iraqis are still dying as a result of war-related bomb damage. According to an Associated Press report dated January 9, 1992, 70,000 Iraqis have died since the end of the war from hardships, such as inadequate medical care and poor food distribution.

16. The estimates were later revised downward. The Pentagon now estimates that about 700 Iraqi tanks and 1,400 armored personnel carriers survived the war. Many of these weapons were used later to quell the Shiite revolt in the south.

5 A Nation in Turmoil

THE PERMANENT CEASE-FIRE

The fighting in Kuwait, it will be recalled, ended by means of the unilateral cease-fire ordered by President Bush effective at midnight EST on February 27 (0800 hrs on February 28 in the desert). Under its terms, Iraq was directed to cease all fighting, accept all U.N. Security Council resolutions, provide information on all sea and land mines in the theater of operations, and release all allied POWs and Kuwaiti detainees. Iraq, which three days earlier had stopped all fighting anyway and had formally agreed to comply with all U.N. Security Council resolutions, offered no objections. It began releasing POWs almost immediately and agreed to furnish the allied authorities with the information they had requested on mines.

The cease-fire may have ended the fighting, but not Iraq's humiliation and punishment. It merely shifted the locale of the anti-Saddam rancor from the battlefield of Kuwait to the U.N. Security Council, where allies loyal to President Bush or greatly intimidated by him began the arduous task of handing Iraq the kind of punishment it would never forget.

As a first step in this process, an interim cease-fire resolution was enacted by the Security Council. It offered Iraq an end to the fighting once it had fully complied with the basic war aims of the allies--in effect the terms imposed by the President on February 27. Additionally, Iraq was directed to rescind its actions purporting to annex Kuwait; to accept in principle its liability for any loss, damage, or injury arising from the invasion; and to begin immediately the return to Kuwait of all property removed from that nation during the Iraqi occupation. The Security Council resolution said nothing of the trade and arms embargoes or other sanctions that had been previously imposed on Iraq. Presumably, these would remain in effect even though the basic reasons for which they had been enacted no longer applied. As for the arms embargo, retaining it at least as long as Saddam Hussein remained in power was a foregone conclusion, the United States having said so repeatedly. The interim cease-fire resolution was approved by the Security Council on March 2 by a vote of 11 for, 1 against (Cuba), and 3 abstentions (China, India, and Yemen). Voting with the majority were Zimbabwe and Ecuador. Both had straddled the issue in the debate, and their final vote had been far from certain.

The ink had hardly dried on the interim cease-fire resolution when the United States began pressing its coalition partners for the preparation of a final document to end the war. Two factors contributed to the U.S. urgency: a desire to bring home the troops, especially the forces deep inside Iraq and in Kuwait, which would have been impractical without the war actually having ended; and frustration, even bitterness, that Saddam Hussein had succeeded in hanging onto power in Baghdad. A set of new tough terms imposed on Iraq, Washington reasoned, could accomplish what the war had failed to do, that is, cause the people of Iraq to rise against Saddam Hussein. In the aftermath of the war, the United States was confronted with many difficult decisions on the future of its military forces in the Gulf and the timing for their withdrawal. Several thousand troops remained in southern Iraq, and technically their withdrawal could not begin until some kind of a U.N. observer force had arrived in the area to supervise the truce and protect the thousands of refugees living there. There was also the need for a military force, preferably Arab, to be organized and stationed in Kuwait to help guarantee the emirate's security. As important as these issues were, they were overshadowed by Washington's other major quandary: What did the future hold for Saddam Hussein in the aftermath of his crushing military defeat? What about the Iraqi people? Would they simply endure his many transgressions or were they likely to take up arms against him?

The document, whose preparation the United States had been urging, ultimately took the form of a mammoth U.N. Security Council

Resolution (Resolution 687). The United States, as its principal author, had hoped to make its terms much harsher, but opposition by other Security Council members, notably China, India, and the Soviet Union, forced a scaling down of the U.S. demands. Still in its final form, the resolution punished and humiliated Iraq severely, forcing it to accept terms not imposed on any other nation in the history of the international organization. "There is a limit to the amount of coercion that one nation can apply on another," protested Iraq's Ambassador at the U.N. But at the end, twelve nations, including the Soviet Union, China, the United Kingdom, and France, voted for the resolution. Cuba voted against it; Yemen and Ecuador abstained.[1]

The resolution (see Appendix L) essentially had two goals: (1) to destroy whatever Iraqi offensive military capability might have survived the war; and (2) to shackle Iraq's economy in such a way as to force the victimized and oppressed Iraqi people to rise in revolt against their leader. In line with the first goal, Iraq was directed to accept the destruction of all its chemical and biological weapons, their research and manufacturing facilities, ballistic missiles with a range of 150 kilometers or greater, and nuclear materials regardless of purpose (civilian or military). To ensure that Iraq's resulting semi-demilitarized status would continue for at least as long as Saddam Hussein remained in power, the resolution reaffirmed also the prohibition against all sales to Iraq of arms and military materiel of any kind.

The economic squeeze on Iraq was to be accomplished by means of two powerful provisions. The first reaffirmed Iraq's liability "for any direct loss, damage, including environmental damage and the depletion of natural resources, as a result of the invasion and occupation of Kuwait," these losses to be paid from a percentage of profits from Iraq's petroleum exports,[2] if and when such exports were approved. The second reaffirmed the continuation of all economic sanctions against Iraq, in the process preventing Iraq from selling its oil, earning foreign exchange, and trading normally, except for foodstuffs. The two economic provisions were designed to hold Iraq hostage until the above military provisions had been fulfilled and/or Saddam Hussein had been removed from office.

As expected, Iraq greeted the resolution with scorn and charges that it was infringing on the country's sovereignty and territorial integrity. The resolution was vindictive and exceeded the authority of the U.N. Charter, protested Baghdad's leading newspapers, and was part of a "worldwide American plan to rule the world" and impose control on the region and its resources. If the United States, they complained, was really interested in enhancing the security of the Middle East, it should demand that all nations (especially Israel and Syria) dispose of their chemical and nuclear weapons and their means of delivery. By imposing these terms only upon Iraq they were exposing it to future aggression and to threats of blackmail.

The U.S. government listened carefully, unsure whether the complaints represented official policy or just a case of the Iraqis letting off steam. On April 13, to the relief of Washington, the Iraqi National Assembly accepted the harsh terms laid out in Resolution 687. "Iraq," admitted its Foreign Minister, "has no choice but to accept."

In retrospect it is appropriate to wonder: Why did Iraq say yes to a resolution so heavily tilted against it? Except for a formal ending of the war and the withdrawal of the coalition forces from the area, the resolution gave Iraq absolutely nothing; even the economic sanctions remained in effect. Under the terms of the resolution Iraq is destined to become a near-demilitarized nation with an economy mortgaged for many years to come.

There are various theories. The most credible concerns the events inside Iraq during March and early April 1991, when the United States came under extraordinary pressure to intervene on behalf of Shiite and Kurdish rebels under attack by troops of Saddam Hussein. An informal U.S.-Iraqi understanding probably did ensue at that time, with Iraq agreeing to accept the U.N. resolution in exchange for a U.S. pledge of noninterference in the rebellions. By accepting the U.N. resolution, Iraq freed the President's hand and made possible the return home and victory celebrations of the men and women who participated in Operation Desert Storm.

March 3 to 22, 1991

REBELLION IN THE SOUTH

As the defeated troops of Saddam Hussein began drifting home from Kuwait and southern Iraq, the news of carnage and defeat arrived with them. Despite the official attempts to mask the reality of the national disaster ("You have faced the whole world, great Iraqis, and you have won," Saddam Hussein had proclaimed), few Iraqis any longer gave credence to the official declarations of the war's "glorious ending." The contrast between the tales of Iraqi heroism on the battlefield, heralded by Baghdad radio and in the print media, and the evidence of humiliation and defeat was all too obvious.

The trauma of Iraq's military debacle was soon augmented by news of renewed fighting, this time in the southern cities of Basra, Karbala, and Najaf, where Iraqi Shiites,[3] encouraged by the anti-Saddam rhetoric of President Bush and by Iran's aspirations for the establishment of a breakaway Shiite republic, began attacking local authorities loyal to President Saddam Hussein. The ranks of the rebels, small at first, swelled within a few days to several thousand by the addition of Shiite soldiers retreating from the front and by pro-Iranian Iraqi exiles[4] armed and supported by Teheran. In its initial phase, the rebellion was clearly directed against Saddam's provincial officials, police, and security forces, but as defiance to the regime spread throughout the Shiite south, clashes between rebel Shiites and Republican Guards loyal to Saddam Hussein became inevitable.

Saddam responded brutally to the challenge, attacking and ravaging the rebels with tanks and helicopters, retaking their strongholds and executing anyone suspected of disloyalty. The rebel troops fought bravely, but in the end, Saddam's superior weaponry prevailed. Basra came under his control on March 12, and a week later the remaining cities in the south were recaptured. When he was finished, much of Basra, the Shiite stronghold of Karbala, and the holy city of Najaf lay in ruins, many of their residential areas, even religious shrines, charred and blasted by mortar shells.

The United States greeted the rebellion in absolute silence, even though some of its best troops were stationed within earshot of the fighting. U.S. reluctance to become involved angered the Shiites. The United States, they protested, had repeatedly urged the people of Iraq to take up arms against their dictator and now that they had done so Washington was remaining uninvolved. Other than a brief statement by President Bush, on March 13, which warned Iraq against the use of helicopter gunships to suppress the rebellion[5]--but which was never enforced--the U.S. silence was deafening. It was all reminiscent of the U.S. posture in 1956, when the United States, after urging the people of Eastern Europe to rise against Soviet oppression, refused to support them militarily when they did attempt the revolt.

In retrospect it is apparent that President Bush found himself totally unprepared for the kind of free-for-all that materialized in the Shiite south, and later in the Kurdish north, in the aftermath of the Gulf war. Yes, he had publicly exhorted the Iraqis to topple their leader, but what the President and his allies had in mind with this call was a "palace coup"--a peaceful changeover in power in Baghdad from one Baathist general to another. The President had no idea that his call for revolt would be taken seriously by more than half the Iraqi population.

Having incited a revolt that had suddenly taken a wrong turn, the President was now ready "to make a correction." It is not in the U.S. national interest for the Shiites to win the rebellion, he advised those who questioned his policy, because a Shiite victory would be synonymous with the "Lebanonization" of Iraq. The Shiites, under the direction and prodding of Iran, were hoping to create an autonomous nation in the south carved from Iraqi territory. Assisting the Shiite rebels would make the United States an accessory in the breakup of Iraq and accountable for the widespread instability and chaos that would follow. A Shiite victory could pose a temptation for Iraq's other neighbors to move in and dismantle big chunks of its territory, much in the same manner that Syria and Israel have done in Lebanon. It was not an issue of abandoning the rebels, explained the President's men. U.S. interests dictated that Iraq remain whole, even if this meant delaying Saddam Hussein's departure from power a bit longer.

There was logic in the President's thinking, but it also failed to answer a key question. If the Iraqi Shiites were determined to establish their own fundamentalist state similar to that of Iran, why did they not rise in revolt during the years of the Iraq-Iran war, when presumably their chances for success would have been brighter? It is a historical fact that Iraq's Shiites remained loyal to Baghdad throughout that war, electing loyalty to their nation over that to their religion. There simply is no evidence that the revolt in the south was prompted by a large-scale Shiite separatist desire. The revolt was driven by anti-Saddam Iraqis (primarily Shiites but also many Sunnis) who, encouraged by the President's words, sensed an opportunity to oust the Iraqi leader in the aftermath of his military disaster in Kuwait.

There was, of course, much more than the threat of Iraq's fragmentation on the President's mind. The President's number one priority in early March 1991 was the return of the troops home. Reengaging the Iraqi forces, first by taking on their helicopter gunships, later by attacking their tanks and artillery and getting involved in a war deep inside Iraq, was the very Vietnam-type scenario that he had promised the American people he would avoid.

REBELLION IN THE NORTH

The President's policy toward the Shiite rebellion was firm and unyielding. Having made up his mind, rightly or wrongly, to stay out of the conflict, he stuck to his policy with stubborn determination. One factor that made it easy for the President to remain unwavering in his position was the almost total absence of television coverage from the front. The few reports on the Shiite rebellion that did filter out of Iraq lacked the drama or ability to arouse grass-roots interest. As a result, much of the American public remained indifferent to the Shiite plight, electing instead to celebrate the victory in Kuwait and the pending return home of the men and women of Operation Desert Storm.

A far more complex situation, however, confronted the President when the Kurds in the north, after unsuccessfully confronting Saddam's army, fled their homes to seek safety in the mountains along the Turkish and Iranian borders. The television images of hundreds of thousands of Kurdish men, women, and children fleeing for life, shivering on snow-covered mountains, many in their bare feet or clad only in makeshift clothing, touched the nation's soul. To be sure, Americans knew precious little of the Kurds, of their seventy-year long struggle for independence or at least a measure of autonomy, and of their recurring persecution at the hands of Iraqis, Turks, and Iranians.[6] But the images of the terrified and helpless refugees were all too powerful for Americans to ignore, raising questions whether their nation might not be in some way responsible for the tragedy.

March 4 to 30, 1991

The Kurdish Rebellion and Defeat

By all accounts, the Kurdish rebellion began on March 4, at about the same time that the Shiites in the south took up arms against Saddam and his regime. The Kurds, with a long history of opposition to Baghdad, did not need much encouragement to act. The news of the Iraqi army's disaster in Kuwait, coupled with the appeals for revolt by President Bush and broadcasts from the "Voice of Free Iraq,"[7] which promised to stand by them "in whatever you carry out and in every step you undertake," made this truly the hour of destiny for the Iraqi Kurds.

With Saddam Hussein busy quelling the Shiites in the south, the Kurdish rebellion at first enjoyed unqualified success, forcing Saddam's troops out of much of Iraqi Kurdistan and freeing the cities of Erbil, Dahuk, and Kirkuk, even threatening briefly the major oil center of Mosul. But it was only a matter of time before the Iraqi leader would turn his fury toward the Kurds. By late March, after crushing the Shiite rebellion in the south, 100,000 of his best troops invaded the north, shelling and bombing Kurdish strongholds, burning villages, and retaking control of the rebel cities. It was not even a contest. It took all of five days for the troops loyal to Saddam (armed with tanks, artillery, and helicopter gunships) to smash the 50,000 or so lightly armed Kurdish army of rebels, army deserters, and militia men. The Kurdish tragedy, however, did not end with the cessation of fighting. In typical Saddam fashion, the strafing of Kurdish areas and the indiscriminate killing of Kurdish civilians continued for several days after all organized rebel resistance had ceased.

March 30 to April 15, 1991

The Exodus to the Mountains

Confronted by the threat of certain extermination at the hands of Saddam's security forces and helicopter gunships, 2 million Kurds left their towns and villages in the north for the safety of the surrounding mountains. By mid-April the refugees had either crossed into Iran, were lined up to enter Iran, or were stranded on the Iraqi side of the Turkish border. While Iran welcomed the fleeing Kurds, Turkey kept its borders closed. Officially, its explanation was that it "did not have the resources to deal with the mass migration." The truth, however, was that Turkey, with 14 million Kurds of its own, did not want the Iraqi Kurds mingling with its own Kurds and in the process reviving talk of a free Kurdistan.

The television images of freezing and starving Kurds, waiting under the harshest of weather and terrain conditions for permission to enter Turkey, shocked Americans. A national debate soon ensued over who was to blame, and whether America could stand by idly while Saddam Hussein's tanks and gunships were raining death and destruction on the Kurdish people. Opinion polls taken during that period exposed the national agony. "Do you think that the United States should try to help the rebels overthrow Hussein?" 769 randomly selected adults were asked on April 3 by a *Washington Post*/ABC News poll. Of those answering the question, 51 percent said no, while 45 percent replied yes.[8]

Increasingly, President Bush too came under criticism for pro-mulgating a policy of rebellion against Saddam Hussein, only to stand by while the Iraqi dictator was ravaging the Shiite and Kurdish communities. Bringing the U.S. troops home, noted the President's critics, and preventing the fragmentation of Iraq were worthwhile objectives, but how could the United States which dispatched half a million men and women to the Gulf to reverse Saddam's invasion of Kuwait, claim that the genocide of the Kurds, by the same Saddam, was none of its business? "Hypocrisy," noted Flora Lewis in her column in the *New York Times*, "is too weak a word for a policy of bombing the daylights out of Iraq and then asserting no responsibility at all for its internal affairs, after calling on Iraqis to overthrow their tyrant." Critics of the President were not calling for a renewed ground war. Their argument was with his reluctance to order Iraq to cease using helicopter gunships and tanks against the Kurds. A similar order, it will be recalled, had grounded all Iraqi fixed-wing aircraft under the terms of the temporary truce that ended the fighting. If grounding Saddam's aircraft was militarily correct, critics wondered, why not ground also his helicopter gunships and tanks?

April 5, 9, and 16, 1991

The President Acts

Stung by widespread criticism that he had abandoned those whom he had personally summoned to revolt against Saddam Hussein, the President finally decided to act. On April 5, after blaming the human tragedy unfolding in and around Iraq "on the brutal and inhumane actions of the Iraqi government,"[9] he ordered U.S. Air Force transport planes to fly over northern Iraq and to drop supplies of food, blankets, clothing, and tents to the stranded refugees. It was the least that the United States could do. Mountains of unused food and clothing were crowding the military warehouses in Saudi Arabia, not to mention the tons of additional provisions en route to the Gulf but no longer needed because of the war's early ending.

Although the humanitarian operation launched by the President's order eventually involved 40 C-130 transport planes, 60 helicopters, and about 100 small tactical vehicles, it barely made a dent. The Kurdish exodus continued, and so did the misery, pain, and hunger of the fleeing refugees. On April 9, even though Iraq had already suspended operations against the rebellious Kurds, the Bush administration did what it should have done five weeks earlier--it ordered Baghdad not to use its military forces in the area of Iraqi Kurdistan (roughly the area north of the 36th parallel). The warning specifically barred the use of any force against the refugees fleeing into Turkey and Iran and included an explicit injunction against the use of fixed-wing aircraft, as well as helicopters.[10]

The purpose of the President's order of April 9 was clearly political, but it also had a diplomatic dimension to it. At home, it was intended to acknowledge America's responsibility for shielding the Kurds from future violation and to deny charges that the United States was standing by idly while a brutal dictator was wiping out an innocent people. But to the government in Baghdad, the order was intended to convey reaffirmation of continued U.S. opposition to the fragmentation of Iraq and commitment to the principle of noninterference in its internal affairs. The dual pledge, the Bush administration hoped, would encourage Iraq to accept Resolution 687 (the resolution ending the Gulf war then under consideration by the U.N. Security Council) and in turn make possible the return home of the men and women of Operation Desert Storm.

The final presidential action involving the Kurdish refugees was again the result of outside influences rather than concerted U.S. policy planning. Applying pressure this time were Turkey (which had come increasingly under pressure to open its borders to the refugees, but had refused) and several members of the European community under the leadership of Great Britain and France. Citing dissatisfaction with the ongoing humanitarian efforts, these nations began lobbying for the establishment of "safe havens" in northern Iraq, where Kurdish refugees would be housed and protected from attacks by Saddam's forces. The move, insisted its sponsors, would be a temporary one; a permanent solution would come later, after Baghdad and the Kurds had an opportunity to reach a political settlement.

To the United States, the establishment of safe havens, especially the requirement for providing troops to protect them, violated the very policies of noninterference in Iraqi affairs and nonfragmentation it had professed for so long. But the plan had the potential of pacifying international public opinion and the promise for transferring it later to the United Nations. On April 16, the United States agreed to participate in the plan. "I have directed the U.S. military," announced President Bush at a news conference on that day,

to begin immediately to establish several encampments in northern Iraq where relief supplies for the refugees will be made available in large quantities and distributed in an orderly way. . . . Adequate security will be provided at these temporary sites by U.S., British, and French air and ground forces.

The safe havens were initially conceived as a dozen or so separate "tent cities," where Kurdish refugees would be housed until conditions had improved for their return home. Environmental factors, however, and Iraq's resistance to the plan ultimately necessitated the creation of a contiguous Kurdish enclave eighty miles long and forty miles deep inside Iraq and along its border with Turkey. A total of 10,000 U.S. ground troops, doctors, engineers, and technical personnel participated in the effort of housing, feeding, and clothing the refugees. The operation, Washington knew, was full of pitfalls. (What if the Kurds, for instance, made the enclave their permanent home or used it as a base for attacking troops loyal to Saddam Hussein?) Not

surprisingly, removing the U.S. troops at the earliest possible time
and replacing them with a U.N.-sponsored force soon became a top
U.S. diplomatic priority. Three months later, with U.N. relief experts
and a police force in place and an allied brigade-sized "residual" force
in Turkey ready to intervene on behalf of the Kurds in the event of
renewed Iraqi violence, the last U.S. and allied troops departed the
Kurdish enclave.

Fragmenting Iraq

Needless to say, U.S. plans for maintaining Iraq's territorial
integrity suffered a major setback with the establishment of the
Kurdish enclave and the restrictions imposed on Iraq's military forces
in the area north of the 36th parallel. Iraq's de facto fragmentation
was confirmed in mid-July 1991, when the last U.S. forces departing
northern Iraq handed over control of their border road blocks and
frontier posts to the Kurdish guerrillas, not to Iraqi police or other
central government authority. Simultaneously, Baghdad was warned
by Washington against attempting to reestablish its control over the
enclave.

Turkey, too, took advantage of the power vacuum created by the
Kurdish rebellion. In a move it claimed was designed to defend
against Turkish Kurds who had taken up arms against the central
government, Ankara carved out for itself a "security zone" inside Iraq.
How long before the Kurdish enclave and/or the Turkish "security
zone" become permanent entities, such as the Palestinian camps in
the Gaza Strip or the Israeli "security zone" in Lebanon? Autonomy
talks, underway between Kurdish rebel leaders and the Iraqi government, could result in a measure of autonomy for the Iraqi Kurds
and in the process reverse Iraq's fragmentation. But the Kurds are
demanding nothing less than full autonomy, secured by their own
militia and guaranteed by the international community, terms that the
government in Baghdad is not likely to allow of its own free will.

THE EFFECTS OF STRATEGIC BOMBING

Rebellion and civil strife were not the only hardships that greeted the people of Iraq in the aftermath of the Gulf war. Their economy and urban infrastructure lay completely devastated, a level of destruction so awesome, so "near-apocalyptic," that it "relegated Iraq to a pre-industrial age." The quotes are from a report by M. Ahtisaari, Under Secretary General of the United Nations, who headed a humanitarian mission to Iraq immediately after the war (see Appendix K).

The level of damage inflicted upon Iraq (it has been variously estimated at between $50 billion and $100 billion) is not surprising, considering the intensity of the forty-three-day allied bombing and the enormous amounts of ordnance that were used. U.S. figures released at the end of the war disclose that nearly 90,000 tons of destructive force was dropped on Iraqi targets during the course of the air campaign. Legitimate military targets were on top of the list, but also struck were hundreds of economic and urban infrastructure "targets" of doubtful worth to the final outcome of the war. By U.S. admission, only the laser-guided weapons, or "smart bombs," proved reliable in that they hit their intended targets 90 percent of the time. All other bombs, of which the United States dropped about 82,000 tons, were only 25 percent accurate. Stating it differently, more than 60,000 tons of bombs dropped on Iraq and occupied Kuwait by U.S. aircraft missed their targets.

The precise number of Iraqi economic and urban infrastructure targets that were struck, even though they contributed only minimally to the final outcome of the war, will never be known. To be sure, a conscientious effort was made by U.S. air-war planners to focus attacks on installations and facilities that supported Iraq's war effort. Still, sufficient evidence exists that punishing Iraq by harming its ability to function as a modern industrial state was also a factor in selecting and attacking targets, especially during the latter stages of the war.

A U.S. human rights group that analyzed the allied bombing has concluded that hundreds of Iraqi civilians lost their lives because of the failure of allied commanders to abide by the "requirements of the laws of armed conflict." Violations cited by the group include the frequent use of daytime attacks on military targets in urban areas (which should have been carried out at night when civilians would be away); the failure to make greater use of "smart" bombs and thus minimize civilian casualties; the often indiscriminate bombing of civilian vehicles on highways, and the destruction of agricultural and water-purification facilities of no value to the war effort.

Next to the human losses suffered at home and at the front, nothing has caused more pain to the people of Iraq than the crippling of its electric-power-generating capacity--reportedly, seventeen of twenty of the largest power plants in the country were either totally destroyed or severely damaged during the air campaign. Without electricity to drive water purification and sewage treatment facilities, to store blood and medicines, or to operate basic equipment in hospitals, health conditions throughout the country rapidly deteriorated. In Baghdad, for instance, untreated sewage was and continues to be dumped directly into the river, which is the source for much of the city's water supply system.

The shortage of clean water is cited by international health experts as the principal cause for Iraq's public health crisis. Conditions, they warn, are deteriorating so rapidly that upward of 120,000 children could die from typhoid fever and other diseases brought on by contaminated food and water and the lack of urgently needed medications.[11] The situation is similarly alarming with respect to the nutritional needs of pregnant women and of lactating mothers.

Agricultural experts who have visited Iraq report widespread malnutrition among children. Iraq's food supply crisis, they note, is deteriorating rapidly, and unless urgent steps are taken, "massive starvation" and widespread famine could result. The Iraqi population is fast approaching the threshold of extreme deprivation, except for those few who can still afford to complement the food rationing distribution system by purchases in the free market.

Massive damage inflicted by allied bombing has affected every aspect of Iraq's urban infrastructure. Oil refineries, telecommunications facilities, transportation networks, all lie in ruins. War-related losses also account for the destruction of half of Iraq's livestock and most of its poultry industry. In the words of Ahtisaari, the U.N. official who visited Iraq in March 1991, unless Iraq's crisis in agriculture and food, water, sanitation, and health are reversed, "food that is imported cannot be preserved and distributed; water cannot be purified; sewage cannot be pumped away and cleansed; crops cannot be irrigated; medicaments cannot be conveyed where they are required."[12]

This level of destruction notwithstanding, in a case of badly twisted logic, the United States is insisting that the economic sanctions imposed against Iraq should be retained, even though the purpose for which they were originally imposed expired long ago. Officially, continuation of the sanctions is needed to ensure that Saddam Hussein complies with the military terms of Resolution 687. Unofficially, however, the economic sanctions are designed to cause such grave economic pain on the people of Iraq as to force them to take up arms against their leader and remove him from office. The trouble with the U.S. policy is that Saddam Hussein and his lieutenants in the Baath party are not suffering from the continuation of the economic sanctions, only the people of Iraq are. Despite the lapse of nearly a year since the war, Iraq continues to endure many of the conditions that a U.N. team described in mid-March 1991 as being "near apocalyptic," with most means of modern life support destroyed or rendered tenuous and with epidemics and famine remaining real possibilities.

To be sure, reacting to these findings, the U.N. Security Council, late in March 1991, did lift sanctions on food supplies and eased existing restrictions on the shipment of certain critical humanitarian goods, such as fuel for trucks and electric generators. But these relaxations notwithstanding, Iraq is confronted in the aftermath of the war with enormous economic problems bearing down on its people. Even before the war Iraq had a debt of $80 billion; now it must bear the additional burden of paying for its own reconstruction and for the devastation that its troops caused in Kuwait. Within the U.S. government there are no feelings of compassion or sympathy for the tragedy confronting the people of Iraq. "You will not find America guilty for Saddam Hussein's invasion and the destruction of his own people," noted Marlin Fitzwater, the President's spokesman, on hearing of the U.N. team's findings. "I reject the argument that somehow there is a guilt associated with the destruction of a war caused by Saddam Hussein."[13]

Technically, deciding whether the economic sanctions against Iraq are withdrawn, relaxed, or retained intact (the latter is the U.S. position) is the responsibility of the U.N. Security Council. Five members of the Council--the Soviet Union, China, Cuba, Ecuador, and Yemen--favor some easing. But the United States is adamant that the sanctions remain and so is Great Britain. British Prime Minister John Major has even threatened to veto any easing as long as Saddam remains in power.

What are the chances that the economic sanctions will help topple Saddam's regime? Slim, at best. Bearing the brunt of the economic hardship caused by the sanctions are the people of Iraq, not the government of Saddam Hussein. Sanctions have given rise to steep inflation, especially in food prices; have caused skyrocketing unemployment; and are hindering the repair of many essential civilian facilities ravaged by the allied bombing.[14] In Baghdad alone, all powerplants and substations were destroyed by the bombing. Although makeshift repairs on many of these installations have been made, final repairs cannot be accomplished until Iraq is allowed to market its oil, earn foreign currency, and purchase the required parts and equipment. Justifiably, the people of Iraq are asking: Is the United States waging economic war against us?[15]

ELIMINATING IRAQ'S WEAPONS OF MASS DESTRUCTION

It will be recalled that by authority of U.N. Security Council Resolution 687, whatever Iraqi weapons of mass destruction survived the war are to be destroyed by the government of Iraq under the direct supervision of the United Nations. Theoretically, this will include all remaining Iraqi stocks of chemical and biological weapons, nuclear materials, and long-range ballistic missiles (those with a range of 150 kilometers or greater), as well as the plants and facilities that have the capability for developing and producing such weapons.

The identification, location, and destruction of Iraq's arsenal of weapons of mass destruction is proving to be a far more complex task than the authors of Resolution 687 ever contemplated. Not surprisingly, a year into the process a great deal still remains to be done. The international organization, never known for speed or efficiency, is finding it extremely difficult to translate words into action. The sheer size of Iraq, its penchant for secrecy, and the difficulties inherent in carrying out on-site inspections of a land the size of California are some of the obstacles cited. Lack of funds is another key impediment, especially the hundreds of thousands of dollars that will be required for carrying out the destruction of Iraq's arsenal of chemical weapons. As for Saddam and his Baathist lieutenants, des-pite their formal acceptance on April 13, 1991, of U.N. Resolution 687, they are fighting the process every step of the way and playing masterful games of hide and seek in a desperate effort to keep as many of their weapons of mass destruction out of the reach of the U.N. inspectors.

Long-Range Ballistic Missiles

This is the only weapons area in which the Iraqis have been forthcoming, probably because the weapons involved were not worth preserving. Their postwar inventory of long-range ballistic missiles, they reported, was sixty-one up-graded Scuds, which they proceeded to destroy dutifully in July 1991 in the presence of U.N. inspectors. The destroyed missiles were known to be inaccurate and unreliable and probably were of no more use to the Iraqis.

Suspicion that there might be more to Iraq's ballistic missile program received confirmation in July 1991, when Iraq admitted to the United Nations that it had built and tested a "supergun" capable of delivering unconventional ordnance to distances of six hundred miles. (Presumably, the weapon is too inaccurate for conventional ordnance.) Largely because of this information, U.N. inspection teams are continuing to roam the Iraqi countryside, for evidence of additional missiles or facilities for their manufacture that Iraq might still be holding. The Bush administration is behind this effort one hundred percent. Iraq, it charges, is hiding large numbers of ballistic missiles and may have retained the capability for developing new such weapons.[16]

Biological Weapons

In its initial declaration to the United Nations, in accordance with U.N. Resolution 687, Iraq denied having any biological weapons or ever producing them. Work at all its five biological research laboratories, it said, had been for peaceful purposes, such as for the production of vaccines. Later, however, Iraq acknowledged that a "food inspection facility" at Salman Pak near Baghdad had actually been a biological weapons facility, capable of producing deadly anthrax.

During the Gulf war, allied military pilots did attack and destroy several Iraqi scientific research facilities, but they abstained from striking sites where biological weapons might have been stored for fear of spreading deadly agents across the country and killing millions. As a result, if Iraq has biological weapons stocks (in violation of the Biological Weapons Convention, which it has signed and ratified), they are largely intact.

Whether Iraq did actually produce such weapons or whether it merely experimented with them has still to be established. U.N. inspectors have as yet to find a stockpile of biological weapons, but have found plenty of evidence of a capacity to produce. Salman Pak alone, U.N. inspectors report, had the capacity for producing more than fifty gallons of deadly anthrax per week, an amount sufficient to devastate an area of nearly a thousand square miles.[17]

Chemical Weapons

Information on how many of Iraq's chemical weapons survived the war is equally marred by uncertainty. Iraq entered the conflict, at least according to the U.S. Central Intelligence Agency, with about 1,000 tons of poisonous chemical agents, much of it loaded in bombs, artillery shells, and rockets. During the war all known chemical production and storage sites were struck by the allies, and most were destroyed or heavily damaged. But undoubtedly, many other production and storage sites (whose locations were not known to the allies) survived the aerial bombardment. The fact that chemical agents never entered combat and the absence of any trace of chemical weapons in the bunkers, storage depots, and other facilities left behind by the fleeing Iraqis in Kuwait suggest that Iraq's chemical weapon losses in the war were much smaller than originally believed.

In reports to the United Nations, which the United States has characterized as falling "short of reality," Iraq has disclosed that it is holding a little over 1,000 tons of lethal and intermediate chemicals, as well as several thousand poison gas weapons in the form of artillery shells, missile warheads, and aerial bombs, almost all stored at the huge Samarra chemical weapons complex west of Baghdad. A great many of these weapons, Iraq noted, are buried under debris from the allied bombing. As for the laboratories and facilities that were used for the development, production and mixing of chemical weapons--a total of about sixteen such facilities--all, says Iraq, were destroyed during the war.

A year after the end of the war, little if anything has been accomplished toward the elimination of the Iraqi chemical weapons arsenal. A U.N. inspection team has visited Samarra repeatedly, but has been unable to verify the accuracy of the Iraqi figures because of health dangers posed from leaking and damaged canisters. Inventorying the entire arsenal of Iraq's chemical weapons--both those that it "declared" and those it is trying to conceal--will be an enormous task. But it will pale in comparison to the next step, namely the actual destruction of the weapons. The U.N. Commission on Iraq simply does not have the funds, equipment, or personnel to do this job right. Even under the best of circumstances, the process will require about three years to accomplish.

Which particular method will ultimately be used to destroy Iraq's chemical weapons has still to be determined. Expropriating an Iraqi chemical plant to break down the deadly liquids is one option. Open-pit burning is another, but it is opposed for environmental and health reasons. The best method, but also the most expensive, would utilize the techniques used on Johnston Atoll, the remote island in the Pacific where the U.S. Army is operating a chemical weapons destruction plant. But the Johnston plant has cost the United States a small fortune to construct and operate, and is also prohibited by law from burning chemical agents of other nations.

Nuclear Materials

Despite irrefutable evidence that Iraq did have a nuclear weapons program, one whose sole purpose was to build nuclear weapons, its government continues to cling to the tale that its nuclear activities were designed for "peaceful" purposes. Under U.S. and U.N. pressure, many aspects of the Iraqi nuclear weapons program are slowly coming to light, but whether these revelations account for the totality of the suspect activities will not be known for years. From the outset, Iraq has played a game of cat and mouse with the United Nations concerning its nuclear weapons program, denying its existence, concealing equipment and materials, and otherwise refusing to divulge much of the requested information.

To be sure, Iraq's nuclear weapons program was much smaller than those of the other nations in the Middle East and South Asia that are known to have developed nuclear weapons--Israel, Pakistan, and India--and was at least three years away from giving Iraq the capability to build a nuclear bomb. (Documents removed from Iraq by U.N. inspectors confirm that beginning with 1988 Iraq invested heavily toward the development of nuclear weapons. Iraqi research efforts, however, were thwarted by "technical questions" and the inability to purchase abroad much of the required equipment.) What makes the elimination of the Iraqi program, however, such an urgent U.S. requirement is the desire to punish Saddam for his Kuwaiti adventure and to remove from his control any and all nuclear capability for future mischief. "It would be intolerable to leave the Iraqis in possession of unknown amounts of enriched uranium and the capacity to produce more of it," wrote the *Washington Post* editorially on July 5, 1991. The United Nations, the United States' partner in this endeavor, has a further reason for wishing to put an end to Iraq's nuclear weapons aspirations. Iraq is a signatory of the Nuclear Non-Proliferation Treaty and as such is prohibited from engaging in nuclear weapons work. The world's nuclear non-proliferation regime would be at risk if Saddam's violations of the treaty were allowed to go unchallenged.

In April 1991, when Iraq made its first report to the United Nations under the terms of Resolution 687, it admitted only to the highly enriched uranium it was known to possess (about ninety pounds' worth, used for peaceful purposes, and under the safeguards of the International Atomic Energy Agency). Later, under the threat of renewed U.S. bombing,[18] Iraq admitted to possessing substantial stocks of low-enriched and natural uranium, laboratories, and three separate programs for uranium enrichment--by gas centrifuge, calutron, and gaseous diffusion. Most of this equipment has been destroyed or is now in the hands of U.N. inspectors, but basic doubts still persist about the exact size of Iraq's weapons-grade uranium stockpile. U.N. inspectors are regularly visiting Iraq's three nuclear centers (at Tarmiya, Tuwaitha, and Al Sharqat), as well many smaller sites where nuclear work is suspected, but except for "securing" the enriched uranium already under the control of the International Atomic Energy Agency and returning it to the Soviet Union, results have been disappointing. Small quantities of plutonium have been found but the vital components of weapons and major stockpiles of weapons-enriched uranium (except for some "traces" observed at the main Iraqi research center[19]) are still eluding them. What makes the U.N. inspectors extremely nervous is the fact that until told otherwise by an Iraqi informant, they assumed that Saddam Hussein had only one uranium enrichment program, while he actually had three. Fortunately for the U.S. side, the three Iraqi uranium enrichment programs were still in a pilot stage when the war started, and no more than five pounds of enriched uranium had been produced from all three of them. But given this intelligence failure, what assurance is there that Iraq does not have additional nuclear-related materials and equipment hidden somewhere within its territory? Short of digging out the entire Iraqi countryside, we will never know.

Early in September 1991, the U.N. Security Council again put pressure on Iraq, by means of a resolution, to be more forthcoming on its weapons of mass destruction. It directed Iraq to cease all attempts to conceal research work on nuclear, biological, chemical, or ballistic missile programs and to give U.N. inspectors complete access to all parts of the country. Iraq was especially warned against interfering with overflights by U.N. surveillance aircraft and helicopters.

NOTES

1. U.S. Department of State, Bureau of Public Affairs, *U.N. Security Council Resolutions on Iraq*, April 1991.

2. Thirty percent of Iraq's future revenues from oil will be used to compensate Persian Gulf victims. The United States had earlier insisted on a 50 percent diversion of oil income for this purpose.

3. The Shiites represent the largest part of Iraq's population (about 55 percent). The remainder are Sunni Kurds in the north and Sunni Arabs in the central provinces of the country.

4. David Ignatius, "A Coup in Iraq: Why It Failed and How It May Yet Succeed," *Washington Post*, July 21, 1991.

5. Under the terms of the interim cease-fire that ended the fighting, Baghdad was not allowed to fly any fixed-wing aircraft but was allowed to use its helicopters to transport personnel. Using these helicopters to blast rebels, the United States maintained, violated the spirit of the cease-fire.

6. There are about 28 million Kurds worldwide, most of them living in an area the size of Pennsylvania, now part of Turkey, Iraq, Iran, and Syria. Half

of the Kurds live in Turkey, the remainder in the other areas. When the Ottoman Empire collapsed at the end of World War I, the Kurds were promised independence, but this never came to pass.

7. U.S. officials have consistently declined to confirm or deny links between the "Voice of Free Iraq" and the Central Intelligence Agency.

8. Richard Morin, "Majority in Poll Says U.S. Ended Attack on Iraq Prematurely," *Washington Post*, April 5, 1991.

9. Presidential Statement, released by the White House, Newport Beach, California, April 5, 1991.

10. Elaine Sciolino, "U.S. Warns against Attack by Iraq on Kurdish Refugees," *New York Times*, April 11, 1991.

11. Nina Burleigh, "Watching Children Starve to Death," *Time*, June 10, 1991. See also Mary McGrory, "The Iraq we Left Behind," *Washington Post*, November 3, 1991.

12. U.N. Report by Under-Secretary General M. Ahtisaari on the humanitarian needs of Iraq, March 20, 1991.

13. Paul Lewis, "United Nations Eases Rules on Food and Fuel for Iraqis," *New York Times*, March 23, 1991.

14. Caryle Murphy, "Iraqis Say Sanctions Hurt the Wrong People," *Washington Post*, July 5, 1991. See also Patrick Clawson, "Sanctions Can't Topple Saddam," *Washington Post*, June 23, 1991.

15. In July 1991, Sadruddin Aga Khan, the U.N. official responsible for overseeing relief efforts in the Persian Gulf, warned that without prompt relief, the food shortages prevailing in Iraq would lead to a catastrophe. Largely because of this and other such warnings, the U.N. Security Council in September 1991, authorized Iraq to sell $1.6 billion in oil to pay for food and war reparations. Iraq is refusing to comply, charging that the mechanisms established by the U.N. resolution for monitoring the oil sales and food distribution violate its sovereignty.

16. R. Jeffrey Smith, "Iraq Continues to Hide Missiles, Bush Tells Hill," *Washington Post*, January 15, 1992.

17. Jill Smolowe, "D-Day? More Like ZZZ-Day," *Time*, August 5, 1991. See also John M. Goshko and Trevor Rowe, "U.N. Panel Describes Iraq's Anthrax Threat," *Washington Post*, August 15, 1991.

18. On August 2, 1991, on the first anniversary of Iraq's invasion of Kuwait, the Senate voted 97 to 2 to support the use of all necessary means to rid Iraq of its chemical and biological weapons and its nuclear research facilities.

19. R. Jeffrey Smith, "Arms-Grade Uranium Believed Found in Iraq," *Washington Post*, January 15, 1992.

6 The Middle East: Status Quo *Ante Bellum*

Taking stock of the Middle East in the aftermath of victory is a challenge in judgment and objectivity. There are three obvious pluses from the war:

- Kuwait has been freed and the West's access to Arabian oil has been preserved.
- Iraqi aggression has been checked.
- Saddam's capability for nuclear blackmail has been thwarted.

There are, however, also many minuses:

- Saddam Hussein is still ruling Iraq.
- Kuwait is still the elitist, absolute monarchy it was before the invasion.
- The proliferation of arms in the region is continuing unabated.
- The region still lacks any semblance of "security arrangements."
- Israel and the Arab states are still divided on the future of the West Bank, the Golan Heights, Jerusalem, and the Palestinians. Chances of agreement are extremely remote.

Throughout the Middle East, it seems, it is business as usual--status quo *ante bellum*.

KUWAIT: JUSTICE AND DEMOCRACY CAN WAIT

Despite the enormous suffering and devastation it endured at the hands of Saddam Hussein's army, Kuwait--the nation America helped liberate--still has few real admirers. Its prewar image as an arrogant, undemocratic nation persists, fueled by media reports on the enormous wealth of a few of its families, their affluent life-style, and the insensitive treatment afforded the many foreigners who perform physical work for them. Officially, very close bonds of friendship link the United States with Kuwait. Still Americans feel detached from the distant nation, judging it to be no more than an oil-rich domain where fortunes can be made. Undoubtedly, television images of young Kuwaitis spending the war in fashionable Mediterranean beach resorts and of the Emir living in opulence in Saudi Arabia while the U.S. Corps of Engineers was restoring his palace have contributed greatly toward the indifferent feelings that most Americans nurture toward the Kuwaitis.

It would, of course, be glaringly unfair to ignore the devastation that the small nation of 2 million (only 35 percent of whom are "legally" Kuwaiti) suffered under Iraqi occupation. For seven brutal months, Iraq dealt with Kuwait as if it was its private serfdom, pillaging and raping its land, looting everything that could be moved, and detaining and torturing its people. The arson, rape, and plunder became outright obscene during the latter days of the war when the Iraqis realized that their days in Kuwait were numbered.

The precise cost of Iraq's pillage of Kuwait has still to be computed. The Kuwait government's preliminary estimate of $100 billion may be a bit too high, but not by much when one considers the enormous devastation caused by the Iraqis to the economy of Kuwait, on its urban infrastructure, and especially on its oil industry. The theft of goods alone probably exceeds $20 billion, including gold bullion and foreign currency stolen from the Kuwaiti treasury; aircraft seized from Kuwait Airways; and museum pieces, cars, computers, and equipment of all types taken by individual soldiers.[1] Theft and devastation became the order of the day, especially during the close of Iraq's occupation of Kuwait, with the retreating troops torching and vandalizing hotels, banks, businesses, hospitals, and even private homes. Perhaps as many as 30,000 Kuwaitis were also taken hostage as part of the final process of plunder and destruction.

In addition to its economic consequences, the devastation of Kuwait's oil industry has also produced the largest ecological disaster in human history. First, Iraq spilled untold tons of oil into the Persian Gulf in a misguided effort to influence U.S. military strategy. When this effort backfired, Iraqi troops set on fire about 700 of Kuwait's 1,100 oil wells, including their associated pipelines and refineries. Hundreds of millions of barrels of oil went up in smoke as a result of this unprecedented act of vandalism. Visitors to the burning oil fields expressed total shock at the level of destruction. The magnitude of the catastrophe, they noted, and its apocalyptic effects (huge columns of choking smoke rising from the horizon; their plumes merging overhead to form a charcoal cloud blocking out the sun) were simply impossible to fathom.

The Ecological Disaster

That the destruction of Kuwait's oil fields has had profound implications on its economy cannot be disputed. The torching of the oil wells, however, has also had major environmental consequences. Kuwait, in whose interest it is to exaggerate the extent of the damage in the hope of receiving a larger restitution from Iraq, considers the oil fires to be the forerunner of a great ecological disaster likely to take decades to undo. The U.S. government does not agree. The ecological damage of the oil fires, it claims, is not nearly as serious as originally believed. The reasons for the U.S. position should be obvious. An ecological disaster resulting from the Gulf war would diminish the luster of the U.S. victory in Kuwait.

Before Saddam's invasion, Kuwait produced 2 million barrels of crude a day, most of which was exported. For nearly a year, while thousands of fire-fighters from around the world struggled to contain the oil fires caused by the retreating Iraqis and to a degree also by allied pilots misfiring,[2] not a single barrel of Kuwaiti oil was exported. Oil production resumed in November 1991, when the last of the burning wells was capped, and Kuwait again is exporting oil although at greatly reduced levels. Perhaps as much as 5 percent of Kuwait's underground reserves of crude oil (estimated before the war at between 90 and 92 billion barrels) went up in smoke or raced unchecked into the Persian Gulf as a result of Iraqi vandalism.

The ecological destruction is persisting. A year after the war, the Kuwaiti countryside is dotted with oil lakes caused by oil escaping from the destroyed wells, while pollution and oily drizzle from the sabotaged fields, has made itself felt for hundreds of miles to the north, south, and east, affecting the quality of life of the residents in these areas and contaminating wildlife, agriculture, and fisheries. Earlier fears that the fires might cause a nuclear winter have been eased, but reports of catastrophic effects hundreds of miles away still persist.

From the very beginning, the United States was aware that large-scale destruction of Kuwait's oil fields would be a likely outcome of the war, Saddam having threatened repeatedly to set them ablaze in the event of an allied thrust into Kuwait.[3] Not wishing to raise doubts about the wisdom of the Gulf war, the United States is now playing down the long-term environmental effects of the disaster. The toxic pollutants released by the fires, it asserts, will not change the weather in the Persian Gulf, nor will they disturb the global climate. Many scientists are critical of this view. Washington, they charge, is attempting to present a positive spin on the greatest pollution event in history for fear that knowledge of its true dimensions will erode the military luster of Operation Desert Storm.

The Political Status Quo

U.S. differences with Kuwait over the level of ecological damage inflicted by the war pale in comparison with the dilemma confronting the United States over Kuwait's form of government, which at best can be characterized as totally anachronistic. Simply stated, unless Kuwait can be coerced by the United States in the aftermath of its victory in the Gulf to begin a process of democratic reforms, history will record that the world's greatest democracy sent half a million of its sons and daughters halfway around the globe to fight a war for the return to power of an absolute monarchy.

The monarchy in question is the Sabah family, which has ruled Kuwait since before the nation achieved independence from Great Britain in 1961. The Sabah family's rule has been consistently autocratic, except for a brief period in the early 1980s when the Kuwaitis were allowed a taste of limited democracy, including a free press. In 1986, however, the Emir put an end to the experiment and ordered the parliament dissolved--reportedly, it had begun to act a lot like the U.S. Congress. The Emir would probably have been content to rule without a parliament, had it not been for pressure exerted on him by reform-minded Kuwaitis and by many of the Western nations that helped him regain his throne. In June 1991 the Emir announced that parliamentary elections would be held in October 1992 (apparently it would require sixteen months to organize elections in Kuwait!) but said nothing of other democratic reforms, such as the lifting of censorship, freedom of speech, and the granting of the right to vote to hundreds of thousands of disfranchised Kuwaitis. Under present law, of the 700,000 Kuwaitis who are technically citizens, only about 65,000 are eligible to vote by virtue of their being male, over 21, literate, and descendants of families living in Kuwait before 1920.[4]

The U.S. government is plainly frustrated by the slow place of political reform in Kuwait, but asserts that there is little it can do to force democratic institutions on the Emir. For one, it does not want to appear to be meddling in Kuwait's affairs. Then there is the matter of Saudi Arabia, whose government is an absolute monarchy not unlike that of Kuwait. Reportedly, the Saudi King has warned the United States against "pressing for democracy in Kuwait."[5] Probably because of the Saudi warnings--the last thing any U.S. administration wants is to offend the proud Saudis--U.S. officials began to soft-pedal their criticisms of the Emir and his government. The United States, they note, did not go to war to transform Kuwait into a nation of Western democratic values. The explanation may be historically correct, but it does tend to reinforce the political status quo and frustrates the hopes of Kuwaitis who had expected, as a minimum consequence of the war, the restoration of the limited democracy they had briefly enjoyed before 1986.

Kangaroo Justice

Despite their own cruel suffering in the hands of Saddam Hussein, Kuwaitis gave the world during the months following their liberation an artful demonstration of their own ability to exert tyranny on people. Dispensing repression this time were not roaming bands of Iraqi soldiers, but young Kuwaitis--many, in fact, members of the

Sabah royal family--bent on punishing those who had "collaborated" with the Iraqi occupation authorities.

Prewar Kuwait, it is recalled, consisted of a privileged elite of 700,000 Kuwaiti citizens and twice that number of noncitizens. Included in the latter category were lifelong residents of Kuwait who were denied citizenship because their ancestors were not among the original settlers of the country; several thousand foreign workers, living in Kuwait temporarily; and about 500,000 "foreigners" residing in Kuwait permanently. It was against this latter group of "foreigners," especially the 400,000 or so Palestinians and others from countries like Jordan, Yemen, and Sudan, who had openly supported the takeover of Kuwait, that the young Kuwaitis sought revenge.

With war passions running high and under the guise of martial law then in effect, the young Kuwaitis spent the early weeks after liberation conducting armed sweeps into Palestinian neighborhoods, abducting, torturing, and beating thousands of "collaborators." Perhaps as many as 350 Palestinians were killed in the process and many of their mutilated bodies dumped on vacant lands, while thousands of others were thrown in jail or rounded up and driven to the border with Iraq, where they were forcibly made to cross--without food, clothing, or even documents--in violation of the Geneva Conventions.

Undoubtedly, many of the "foreigners," especially those of Iraqi extraction, did collaborate with the occupation forces. But there is no evidence that *all* or even most of them did. The great majority of the targets of the Kuwaiti witch hunt were not collaborators at all, but simple Palestinians (some businessmen, others middle-class professionals) who carried on with their lives under the occupation, their only crime being that the Palestinian Liberation Organization, which they all supported, had sided with Saddam Hussein in his Kuwaiti venture. Neither could the thousands of Palestinians who had served in the Kuwaiti army be accused of having collaborated with the Iraqi authorities. Many of these former Kuwaiti soldiers had been captured by the Iraqis, kept in detention camps, and then released at the end of the fighting. But because they were of Palestinian ancestry, they were denied readmission to Kuwait and were abandoned in Iraq to manage for themselves.

How did the U.S. government react to the Kuwaiti kangaroo justice being dispensed under the very noses of its troops? With extreme frailty, for fear of embarrassing the Emir! The widespread abuses would probably be continuing to this day had it not been for several human rights organizations, U.S. and foreign, that took it upon themselves to expose the emirate. Especially targeted by these organizations were Kuwait's kangaroo courts, which, under the cloak of martial law still in effect months after the U.N. coalition had freed Kuwait, showed "a Saddam Hussein-like disrespect for human rights and due process,"[6] meting out harsh and arbitrary punishment for alleged collaboration. (In a highly publicized case, a young man was sentenced to fifteen years in jail for wearing a nightshirt with the image of Saddam Hussein imprinted on it.) On May 27, the international protests finally produced results when the Emir ordered the armed vigilantes to cease persecuting the Palestinians; a second order on June 25, 1991, lifted Kuwait's martial law and disestablished its kangaroo courts.

To sum up: Seven months after it was surprised by Saddam's army, Kuwait was free again and its Emir restored to his throne. But Kuwait can hardly be judged a Gulf war success story. Its territory was brutalized by the war, and a giant war-induced ecological disaster is threatening its role as one of the world's largest oil exporters. To the United States, which championed Kuwait's independence and freedom, the emirate is increasingly becoming a source of political embarrassment because of its anachronistic government, the gross human rights violations of its citizens, and its unyielding insistence on the maintenance of the political status quo.

ARMS PROLIFERATION CONTINUES UNABATED

On more than one occasion during war the Bush administration let it be known that once the shooting had stopped, it would use its influence to end the pointless and resource-draining accumulation of arms in the Middle East. The administration never spelled out its precise plans, but the prevailing view in Washington was that for the Middle East to have a chance of lasting peace, two goals would have to be met: the proliferation of *weapons of mass destruction* (nuclear, chemical, and biological) in the region would have to stop; and the flow of *conventional* arms, especially those of a destabilizing nature (i.e., bombers, tanks, long-range missiles, etc.) would have to be "severely restrained." The ultimate goal, of course, was the emergence of a stable and secure Middle East, where no nation would feel at risk because of the arms arsenals of its neighbors.

The first clue that things would not quite work out this way came immediately after the war, when in March 1991 the President addressed a joint session of the Congress. To the surprise of many who had hoped that he would use this opportunity to announce plans for curbing *all* weapons proliferation in the Middle East, conventional as well as unconventional, the President limited his remarks only to *weapons of mass destruction*, pointedly omitting reference to conventional arms control from his postwar agenda.

Reopening the Middle East Arms Bazaar

By neglecting to address the crucial issue of conventional arms control, the President in effect was admitting that, contrary to earlier expectations, national interests dictated the continued flow of arms into the region. American arms, explained administration spokesmen, were needed in the aftermath of the war to fulfill a number of important national security objectives: to reward Arab allies for their loyalty in the war, to fill the military vacuum resulting from the departure of the American forces from the area, and to satisfy the increasing demands by many oil-rich Middle Eastern nations for fighter-bombers, helicopters, and many of the other weapons that helped defeat Iraq. In short, the flow of American weapons into the Middle East was here to stay, notwithstanding their destabilizing effect and the risks they posed.

The main thrust of the President's address and subsequent announcements of large-scale arms sales to Egypt, Israel, and Saudi Arabia was reminiscent of the prewar Middle East arms bazaar days, when any nation with hard currency on hand had access to U.S., French, British, Chinese, and even Soviet arms. By offering its sophisticated and highly praised weapons to the nations of the region, the United States was ignoring the perils of rearming the Middle East, a region known for its large craving for armaments--between 1982 and 1989 alone, Saudi Arabia, Iraq, Iran, and Syria squandered about $120 billion in conventional arms purchases[7]--and was making it possible for a future Saddam Hussein to again become the bully of the region by amassing an enormous arsenal of conventional arms.

Stung by criticism of his policy in the Congress and the media, the President in May 1991 decided to make a correction. The new policy (the "Middle East Arms Control Initiative") did not stop the movement of *all* conventional arms into the Middle East, as some in Congress had hoped, but it did include a pledge to the effect that the United States would work to "restrain destabilizing conventional arms build-ups in the region." But the initiative included also another pledge--and it is here that it all gets vague and confusing--in which the United States agreed to support the right of any nation in the region to acquire "the conventional capabilities it legitimately needs to deter and defend against military aggression."[8] In other words, the arms bazaar would remain wide open.

Nuclear Arms Control: A Washout in the Middle East

In contrast to the bumpy reception of his conventional arms policy, the President's plans for curbing nuclear, chemical, and biological weapons in the Middle East won him much praise at home. The United States, proclaimed the President, supported the ultimate establishment of a nuclear-weapons-free zone for the Middle East and to this effect was calling upon all states in the region to implement a verifiable ban on the production and acquisition of weapons-useable nuclear material, to accede to the Non-Proliferation Treaty, and to place their nuclear facilities under the safeguards system of the International Atomic Energy Agency.

But, in the Middle East where the issue ultimately will be decided, the Presidents's plans for restricting weapons of mass destruction turned out to be a washout. Israel, as the region's most powerful nation and the only one with a sizeable nuclear arsenal and a capacity to produce ballistic missiles, expressed puzzlement over the U.S. emphasis on weapons of mass destruction ahead of conventional arms. Conventional arms are the major source of instability in the Middle East, it pointed out, and therefore the primary focus of future arms control arrangements in the region should be on these arms. The reasons for Israel's position should be obvious. Israel is at a military disadvantage vis-a-vis the Arab states in conventional arms, therefore its insistence that such arms be controlled first.

The Arab states are similarly opposed to the President's arms-control plans, but for different reasons--notably Israel's large nuclear arsenal, which reportedly consists of more than a hundred nuclear warheads. The plan is unrealistic, they complain, because it only restricts the production of new nuclear materials, not existing holdings. Acceptance of the plan would legitimize Israel's status as the only nuclear-weapons power in the region and would lock the Arab states in a position of military inferiority in relation to Israel. The President's proposals, in the view of Arabs, have no chance of approval without ironclad assurances that Israel's nuclear stockpile will be phased out.

The two sides also differ sharply on the concept for a Middle East nuclear-weapons-free zone, even though they both subscribe to the idea. Before discussions can even begin on this subject, assert the Arab states, Israel must agree to join the Nuclear Non-Proliferation Treaty and to place all its nuclear installations under the safeguards system of the International Atomic Energy Agency. For Israel, the problem is different. A nuclear-weapons-free zone cannot come into being in the region until the Arab states recognize Israel as a legitimate state. The prerequisite first step, therefore, is for the Arab nations to recognize Israel and then to sit down with its representatives in formal negotiations to work out the necessary arrangements for the establishment of the zone.

Rearming the Middle East

The chances that the United States will ultimately succeed in realizing the objectives of the Presidents's Middle East Arms Control Initiative are extremely poor. For one thing, no practical formula exists for bridging the enormous nuclear imbalance between Israel and the Arab states, and until this imbalance has somehow been rectified, the Arab nations will continue to seek their own security by means of chemical arms, clandestine nuclear research, and the purchase of sophisticated conventional arms (from any nation willing to sell them). U.S. success is also frustrated by the fact that four other nations are equally responsible for exporting into the Middle East conventional arms, many of them of the "destabilizing" variety. The four--the Soviet Union, China, Great Britain, and France--along with the United States, normally account for almost 90 percent of all weapons sold to the region.

Prompted by the President's initiative and a parallel proposal by French President Francois Mitterand, the five major arms exporters have developed "rules of restraint" for their future arms activities in the Middle East. No major breakthrough is expected from this effort, despite official acknowledgment by all concerned that "indiscriminate transfers of military weapons and technology contribute to the instability" of the region. Respective national interests, economic considerations, and aggressive lobbying by weapons producers at home will ultimately tip the scales in favor of continued arms sales. In the meantime, as proof that something positive will result from their efforts, the five nations have pledged to keep each other advised of arms sales into the region and are now collaborating with the United Nations in the establishment of an "arms transfer register."

In the United States, the scales have already been tipped in favor of arms sales. Late in July 1991, at about the same time that its diplomats were meeting in Paris with representatives of the other four arms-exporting nations to establish guidelines for "restraint" in arms sales to the Middle East, the United States announced a proposed sale of $365 million worth of high-technology bombs and missiles to Saudi Arabia.[9] The announcement, the sixth such deal of arms sales to the Middle East since the end of the war, brought the total value of such sales to $6 billion. Earlier the United States had announced sales of 20 Apache attack helicopters to the United Arab Emirates and 8 to Bahrain; 46 F-16 jets and 80 air-to-ground missiles to Egypt; 18 aircraft to Kuwait; about $1 billion worth of spare parts to Saudi Arabia; and the transfer of 10 F-15 fighters to Israel, along with a pledge of more than $200 million in new aid for Israeli antimissile research.[10] A classified request for an additional $18 billion in sales reportedly has been sent to the Congress to arm Egypt, Saudi Arabia, Turkey, the United Arab Emirates, and Bahrain as a reward for their loyalty in the war, but also to replenish equipment and materiel consumed in the fighting.

The lack of restraint in U.S. arms sales is also being demonstrated by France, Great Britain, China, and the Soviet Union, although the latter's weapons may no longer be marketable in light of their less than spectacular performance during the war. France's principal candidates for export include the Exocet missile, truly a lethal and much-sought-after weapon; Britain's, the Tornado fighter; and China's, the Silkworm antiship missile. China, with a history of nonparticipation in multilateral efforts designed to limit dangerous nuclear sales and long-range missiles, appears to be the most aggressive peddler of arms. According to newspaper reports, it has already concluded deals to sell to Pakistan a nuclear-capable missile and to Algeria a reactor capable of producing fuel for nuclear weapons. China is also equipping Syria with surface-to-surface missiles with a range of nearly 400 miles. From Damascus such missiles would be able to reach all of Israel, as well as most of the territories of Turkey, Iraq, Saudi Arabia, and Egypt.

GULF "SECURITY": AS ELUSIVE AS EVER

From the very outset of its military buildup in the Gulf, the United States took the position that its military involvement in the region was only temporary, and that once the war had ended its troops would leave and the military involvement would also end. "We have no intention of maintaining a permanent ground presence on the Arabian peninsula, once Iraq has been ejected from Kuwait and the threat has receded," declared Secretary of State Baker in his testimony before the House Foreign Affairs Committee on February 6, 1991. According to U.S. plans, responsibility for the security of the Gulf in the postwar period was to rest with an Arab peacekeeping force made up of the six Arab Gulf states plus troops from Egypt and Syria, with the United States contributing by means of an enhanced naval presence, regular joint training exercises, and the prepositioning of equipment and materiel (for later use, should an emergency arise).

At home, the policy enjoyed broad support and for a while the Arab states, too, appeared to subscribe to it, even making plans in February and March 1991 for the establishment of a Pan-Arab peacekeeping force to take over security once American and Western forces had departed the region. But as the guns of war were silenced and the Arab nations reverted to their old regional rivalries and quarrels, hope for a regionwide security regime quickly faded and an "America will again rush to our defense" mentality began to take hold throughout much of the region. Before long, Egypt and Syria, the two Arab states with the largest forces in the war, withdrew their troops from the Gulf.

To the utter frustration of Washington, most Arab states appear to have lost interest in regionwide arrangements, preferring instead to forge bilateral agreements with the United States, as long, that is, as such bilateral arrangements do not impose upon them security responsibilities beyond their territory. The departure of all U.S. troops from the area is now favored by all Arab states, and even Saudi Arabia seems to be distancing itself from Washington when it comes to issues of "regional" security. Kuwait is the only exception. About 2,000 U.S. personnel are still stationed in the emirate (it wants no Arab soldiers stationed on its soil) as a guarantee of its security and as a U.S. "deterrent presence" in the Gulf. Kuwait has also agreed to accept the prepositioning of U.S. equipment and materiel and to allow U.S. forces to conduct military exercises on its territory.

Washington is reacting with caution to the sudden change in Arab plans, but it, too, is abandoning hope that a strong regionwide security regime can ever be established. Officially, statements such as "progress is being made" and "agreements will require months of tedious negotiations" are being offered to conceal the U.S. disapppointment. Since the end of World War II, the United States has been frustrated in its search for a powerful ally to take over the protection of the Gulf. Until the early 1970s Great Britain policed the area. Later Iran (the Shah) and Saudi Arabia assumed this role. The Iranian revolution, however, eliminated Iran, and the Iraqi invasion demonstrated Saudi Arabia's inability to deter regional aggression.[11] For the United States, the search for security arrangements to defend the Gulf and its precious resources is proving extremely futile, the prestige and victory over Iraq notwithstanding.

MISSION IMPOSSIBLE:
SETTLING THE ARAB-ISRAELI CONFLICT

On numerous occasions before and during the war, the President had pledged that once Iraq had been forced out of Kuwait, the United States would be fully engaged in attempting to resolve the Arab-Israeli conflict. True to his word, the President restated this pledge in his March 6, 1991, address to Congress ("Our commitment to peace in the Middle East does not end with the liberation of

Kuwait. . . . The time has come to put an end to the Arab-Israeli conflict.") Then he promptly dispatched his Secretary of State to the Middle East to get the process going.

By placing the United States squarely in the midst of the Arab-Israeli breach, the President was reacting to a highly optimistic administration assessment of the postwar situation in the Middle East. The assessment assumed erroneously that the United States, having won the war, would now be able to exert greater influence on the states of the region in matters affecting their future relations and security. It also assumed, again without basis, that a change in Arab and Israeli perceptions had resulted from the war, including a desire to set aside old antagonisms and to resolve differences. Both sides, after all, had confronted Saddam Hussein--the Arabs on the battlefield, Israel by its restraint in the face of Iraqi missile attacks-- and it was in this convergence of security interests that the administration saw a "window of opportunity" for an Arab-Israeli peace.

Status Quo *Ante Bellum*

The truth is, of course, that the Gulf war did not change the region's geopolitical makeup one iota, nor did it contribute to a new spirit of cooperation and goodwill between Israelis and Arabs. In the aftermath of the war, Israel is still angered over the Arab refusal to acknowledge its existence, and the Arab states still persist in regarding Israel as an illegal entity, one that has forced its way into the region and occupied its land.

What made the administration believe that the war had improved prospects for peace in the Middle East is still a mystery. The war, if anything, has increased mutual suspicions between Arabs and Jews, and the region is now no more peaceful or secure than it was before Iraq's invasion of Kuwait. In the Israeli-occupied lands, violence and strife persist, and Israel, to the consternation of Arabs and the U.S. government, too, is continuing to expand its settlements on the West Bank. Even the results of the war are being disputed by the two sides. In the opinion of the Arab states, Israel has gained the most from the war, since Iraq, the only nation able to threaten it militarily, has been crushed. For their part, the Israelis see the Arabs as winners, because of the close U.S.-Arab military ties forged during the fighting and the U.S. military arms assistance flowing into Arab hands since the end of the war. And both sides, the Arabs and the Israelis, expect the United States, as a result of their respective wartime contributions, to pressure the other on their behalf (for the Arabs, pressure on Israel to settle the Palestinian problem; for the Israelis, pressure on the Arabs to end their hostility toward Israel.)

That the odds are formidable against a dramatic breakthrough in settling the Arab-Israeli conflict hardly needs to be elaborated here. At issue are four pieces of land--the West Bank, Gaza, the Golan Heights, and East Jerusalem--which Israel holds as a result of its 1967 victory over the Arabs. Israel is not about to give up these lands, which is what the Arabs want, no matter what the incentive. These lands belong to the Land of Israel,[12] it asserts, and are needed if its sons and daughters are to live in freedom. As for the Arabs, any hope of reclaiming the disputed lands by force would be suicidal--Israel is a nuclear power; none of the Arab states is--thus their demands through the years for an international peace conference under the auspices of the United Nations to "end the Israeli occupation of the Arab territories and to ensure the national rights of the Palestinian people" in accordance with U.N. Resolutions 242 and 338. These, it will be recalled, are the "peace for land" resolutions adopted by the international organization many years ago, which have since been gathering dust because of the complete intransigence of both sides.

When it comes to the future of the disputed lands, the two sides find little to agree on. Note, for instance, the respective views of Israel and of the Arab states concerning U.N. Resolution 242. This resolution, adopted in November 1967, calls for the "withdrawal of Israeli armed forces from the occupied territories" but also acknowledges "the sovereignty, territorial integrity and political independence of every state in the area, and their right to live in peace within secure and recognized boundaries." According to Israel, Resolution 242 has been distorted by the Arabs. The goal of this resolution is to establish a just and durable peace between the parties, not to provide the Palestinians with a homeland. The resolution, contends Israel, makes no reference to Palestinian self-determination, or to an international peace conference, or to the right of the Palestine Liberation Organization to be represented. The resolution demands only that Israel's armed forces be withdrawn, not its administration or other aspects of sovereignty. As for the "land for peace" requirement of the resolution, it has already been fulfilled by Israel's withdrawal from the Sinai Desert as a result of the 1978 Camp David accord.

As expected, the Arab interpretation of Resolution 242 is entirely the opposite. Resolution 242 *is* land for peace, they assert, and a reaffirmation by the international community that it is inadmissable to acquire territory by war (which Israel has done). Israel must withdraw from all occupied lands, including the West Bank, Gaza and the Golan Heights. Then, and then only, will the Arab states end their belligerence toward Israel and accept it as a state in the region.

The "Breakthrough"

Late in July 1991, after months of prodding, cajoling, and pressuring all parties, the United States and the Soviet Union announced the convening in October 1991 of a Middle East peace conference (which subsequently was held in Madrid, Spain.) The announcement, made in Moscow during the President's visit to the Soviet capital, threw in an extra incentive to ensure Israel's participation in the process (which until that time had been uncertain), a promise by the Soviet Union that it would offer diplomatic recognition to Israel if it agreed to attend. Two major compromises were made on the road to the announcement, both incidentally to appease Israel: a provision that the United Nations, the United States, and the Soviet Union would have only a minimal role at the conference; and that the proposed talks between Israel and Syria, Lebanon and Jordan would be "direct." Israel ultimately did agree to participate in the conference, but only after its demands regarding Palestinian representation were accepted by all concerned. Palestinians at the conference, it insisted, could not be associated with the Palestine Liberation Organization or live in East Jerusalem. The latter requirement highlighted Israel's absolute refusal to even discuss the future status of Jerusalem.

Why is the Bush administration placing its prestige on the line with an issue that is simply impossible to resolve? The answer should not be difficult. After the Kurdish tragedy, the destruction caused on Kuwait and the Gulf region by the war, and Saddam's tenacious hold on power, the administration badly needs a diplomatic victory, one that it can point to with pride as a positive result of the war. By bringing Israel and its Arab enemies face to face at the bargaining table, it is hoping that negotiations would generate their own momentum, and perhaps--perhaps--the two sides will find a way to free themselves from the shackles of the status quo. But that assumes that both sides are genuinely ready for peace and compromise, when much of the evidence suggests that Arabs and Israelis accepted the U.S. plan merely to improve their standing with Washington, or out of fear of the consequences of defying President Bush. Certainly, Israel has no incentive to participate in a peace process, if the sole purpose of the negotiations is (as the Arabs maintain) to establish a date for the withdrawal of its military forces from the occupied lands.

SADDAM HUSSEIN REMAINS IN POWER

In survey after survey taken since the end of the war, Americans have voiced frustration that Saddam Hussein, despite the massive U.S. military force applied against him, his defeat on the battlefield in Kuwait, and the Kurdish and Shiite rebellions, is still the man in charge in Iraq. A survey of 1,000 Americans, for instance, sponsored by Americans Talk Security and conducted between June 23 and July 1, 1991, found that the biggest lingering doubt Americans felt about the war was its failure to remove Saddam Hussein from power, with 79 percent of those responding stating that "they worried a lot or all the time" about the Iraqi leader's continued hold on power. This, even though the removal of Saddam Hussein was not a U.S. objective in the war.

Except for a handful of Middle East experts, few Americans before August 2, 1990, had an opinion on Saddam Hussein one way or another, or even knew who he was. Before he ventured into Kuwait, Saddam had not been America's enemy; in fact Presidents Carter, Reagan, and Bush (during the first year of his administration) had regarded Saddam as a friend of sorts, appeasing him and relying on him to keep Iran's brand of Islamic radicalism in check. During Iraq's war with Iran, the United States even extended a helping hand to Saddam, providing him with intelligence data on Iranian troop movements and on the status of important Iranian targets. To be sure, Washington knew all along that Saddam was a bully and an assassin and that he had used chemical weapons against his own Kurdish people in 1988, but the strategic importance of his nation and the need to check the spread of Islamic fundamentalism in the end prevailed. Washington looked the other way whenever Saddam misbehaved, such as when an Iraqi aircraft accidentally (?) attacked the U.S.S. *Stark*, killing 37 American sailors. The United States also looked the other way when Saddam began massing troops to invade Kuwait, with our own Ambassador April Glaspie telling him on July 25, 1990, that the United States was eager to improve relations with him, practically assuring him that it would not interfere in his border conflict with Kuwait.[13]

That Saddam Hussein has managed to remain in power despite his humiliating defeat in Kuwait, the postwar rebellions in his country, and the severe punishment being meted out against him by U.N. Resolution 687 is indeed a minor miracle. Any other political leader who so badly miscalculated the political will and military power of his enemy and who single-handedly caused the destruction of his country would have been swept from power long ago.

But Saddam Hussein is unlike other political leaders. He is a survivalist, who draws strength from a highly disciplined party at home, an army personally loyal to him, and a network of secret police and informers that penetrates every corner of Iraqi society.[14] Kuwait was not the first instance in which the Iraqi leader placed his own ambition above the interests of his people. Throughout the 1980s, he led his nation in a senseless war against Iran, taking enormous economic losses, sacrificing hundreds of thousands of Iraqi youths, and gaining absolutely nothing in return. When that war ended, the party, the army, and the secret police again rallied around him, pledging their support and extolling him as a conquering hero. Any reasonable leader after fighting an eight-year war would have focused on the reconstruction of his country and the healing of its wounds. But, not Hussein. Within two years of the cease-fire with Iran, he launched a new foreign adventure (Kuwait), aspiring this time to become the custodian of nearly a fifth of the world's oil reserves.[15]

To President Bush, who spent a great deal of energy and effort during the war in verbally harassing Saddam Hussein, comparing him to Adolf Hitler, and reminding Americans of the "man's" cruelty against his own people, Saddam's survival in power and his constantly improving domestic situation since the war come as a major disappointment. Officially, Saddam's removal from power is not a U.S. policy goal, but unofficially, the administration continues to pressure the Iraqi military and Baath ruling party to oust Saddam, by threatening to keep Iraq isolated and the economic sanctions against it intact as long as he remains in power.

Why the national obsession with Saddam? The Iraqi leader no longer threatens anyone, nor are his authoritarian government and his cruelty against his own people unique in the world. (There are plenty of Saddams around.) The drive to remove the Iraqi leader is directly linked to Operation Desert Storm and the administration's fixation on having the Gulf war recorded in history as a great American success story. The United States cannot claim to have confronted evil and won, so long as Saddam Hussein continues in power in Baghdad and turns up his nose defiantly at the victors.

THE NEW WORLD ORDER

No discussion of the postwar Middle East can be considered complete without a brief mention of the President's "new world order." The order, after all, is the central theme of the President's foreign policy and one upon which he hopes to build a better tomorrow.

The President's concept for a new world order originated early in 1990 in the aftermath of the crumbling of the Iron Curtain. It was to acknowledge the end of the Cold War and to herald the beginning of a new era of cooperation and peace between the superpowers. When Saddam Hussein invaded Kuwait, the new world order did not quite fit the scheme of things, but the President, searching for a rationale to justify America's military involvement 7,000 miles away from home, modified the concept to make it applicable also to the Middle East. A new opportunity exists for a new world order in the Middle East, he noted on the very evening that he directed the coalition forces to begin the air campaign against Iraq, one "where the rule of law . . . governs the conduct of nations."

The many ambiguities surrounding the concept, especially as it applied to the Middle East, forced the President later to clarify his concept. There are four principles, he noted, that the nations of the region, working together under the United Nations, should use to deter aggression and to achieve peace and prosperity. The principles are the peaceful settlement of disputes, solidarity against aggression, reduced and controlled arsenals, and a just treatment of all peoples. Missing among the President's principles, however, were the key objectives that had guided U.S. foreign policy throughout the twentieth century: the quest for freedom and democracy, human rights, and the self-determination of peoples everywhere. By their omission, was one to understand that they did not belong in the new order being established for the Middle East?

It would serve no useful purpose to repeat here the evidence presented elsewhere in this chapter. Throughout the Middle East, it is business as usual on the political, economic, and territorial issues that have divided the peoples of the region--with a new world order nowhere on the horizon.

NOTES

1. Shawn Tully, "Who Will Rebuild Kuwait?" *Fortune*, March 25, 1991.

2. Jennifer Parmelee, "Environmentalists Survey the Blackened Wasteland that was Kuwait," *Washington Post*, December 20, 1991.

3. Eugene Linden, "Getting Blacker Every Day," *Time*, May 27, 1991. See also Jack Anderson and Dale Van Atta, "Still No Sun in Kuwait," *Washington Post*, July 21, 1991.

4. Michael Kramer, "Kuwait: Back to the Past," *Time*, August 5, 1991.

5. Editorial, "Postwar Kuwait," *Washington Post*, May 19, 1991.

6. Editorial, "Kuwait's Kangaroo Courts," *Washington Post*, June 23, 1991.

7. Editorial, "Disarming the Gulf," *New York Times*, March 2, 1991.

8. The White House, Office of the Press Secretary, "Fact Sheet on Middle East Arms Control Initiative," May 29, 1991.

9. R. Jeffrey Smith, "Administration Proposes Arms Package for Saudis," *Washington Post*, July 30, 1991. According to media reports of January 1992, the Bush administration is planning to sell about 24 F-15E fighters to Saudi Arabia, as the first stage of a multiyear deal ensuring that all warplanes in the Saudi air force are American-made.

10. "U.S. Arms Transfers to the Middle East Since August 2, 1990," FACTFILE, *Arms Control Today*, June 1991.

11. David O. Smith, "The Postwar Gulf: Return to Two Pillars?" *Parameters*, Summer 1991.

12. Ze'ev B. Begin, "The Likud Vision for Israel at Peace," *Foreign Affairs*,

Fall 1991.

13. Ken Coates, ed., *Third World War* (Nottingham, U.K.: Russell Press, 1991), p. 35.

14. Saddam himself is the President of Iraq, the Commander-in-Chief of its armed forces, and the Chairman of the Revolutionary Command Council.

15. Elaine Sciolino, *The Outlaw State: Saddam Hussein's Quest for Power and the Gulf Crisis* (New York: Wiley, 1991), p. 15.

Epilogue

During January and February 1991, the United States, with the active support of a dozen other nations, defeated in battle the armed forces of Iraq, a nation of 17 million led by the thoroughly inept Saddam Hussein. The superior and highly disciplined forces of the U.N. coalition proved too much for Saddam's troops, exhausted from an eight-year war with Iran and demoralized by inferior leadership and poor logistics. On the field of battle, Baghdad's troops performed like the fourth-rate military power that they were, a far cry from the highly armed and disciplined force that Saddam claimed to have under his command.

As for the Iraqi President, reputed to be a cunning and accomplished leader, the Kuwait crisis exposed him for what he really was: a callous tyrant totally inept in the ways of international diplomacy and military strategy. Not only did he allow himself to be drawn into a disastrous war with the United States, but he compounded this error by adopting a strategy for confronting the superior U.S. forces that was nothing short of moronic. On February 23, 1991, Saddam Hussein committed his biggest blunder yet when he summarily rejected the President's ultimatum. By his refusal, the Iraqi leader squandered his last remaining chance for salvaging his army from Kuwait, an error that probably cost his nation 100,000 men. Any rational leader, aware of the destitute morale and condition of his troops, would have embraced the offer the very moment it was offered.

Saddam's diplomatic and strategic miscalculations during the Gulf war are legion. He blundered when he decided to swallow Kuwait whole, instead of nibbling at its edges and camouflaging his aggression as a border dispute with a neighbor. He blundered when he moved his forces toward the Saudi border, giving the nervous Saudis the impression that their kingdom was next on the Iraqi's agenda. And he blundered in a big way when he assumed that his patrons, the Soviets, would support his aggression, that the United States would ignore it, and that Arab brotherhood would prevail in any confrontation with the West.[1]

But if Saddam Hussein miscalculated, so did President Bush. The President erred when he elected to confront Saddam's aggression by means of a *strategy of force*, rather than by means of diplomacy and accommodation. And he misjudged the Iraqi leader's intentions when he assumed that the presence of a large U.S.-led military force in the Gulf and the threat of war would compel him to evacuate Kuwait. The war in which thousands died and billions of dollars were wasted began for all practical purposes at the moment that the President elected to pursue a military solution. The military force that he had hoped would avert war, made war all but inescapable.

From day one of the crisis, the President pursued his strategy of force with unyielding determination. He drew a line on the sand, dispatched more than 500,000 U.S. troops to the Gulf, and coerced the U.N. Security Council to authorize the use of force for the purpose of freeing Kuwait. It was all an exceedingly complex undertaking, and one that the President and his Secretary of State carried out with exceptional skill and devotion. But despite the enormous diplomatic effort involved in organizing and orchestrating a military solution, only once during the entire seven-month prewar period did the President offer to meet the Iraqi leadership in direct face-to-face diplomatic negotiations.

By electing to pursue a strategy of force and rejecting the potential for diplomacy, the President in effect proclaimed to the world that the strong and powerful have no need to negotiate, because they can solve disputes by the use of arms. Sanctions and diplomacy would have forced Iraq to ultimately leave Kuwait, and would have accomplished the desired result without the enormous destruction and loss to life caused by the war. But the President ignored this evidence. There is no room for negotiations, he asserted, in the process backing himself into a corner from which war was the only possible alternative. His emphasis on a strategy of force denied him the opportunity to pursue peaceful channels or to explore areas of possible compromise. Even after the war started, there were plenty of signals from the other side for a negotiated settlement, but the President again refused to explore a diplomatic solution. Had the President shown some flexibility, Saddam might also have been persuaded to act more responsibly himself. But the two leaders never understood each other. Each called the other a liar. To Bush, Saddam was another Hitler, an aggressor, and one that had to be stopped. To Saddam, Bush was the leader of a Zionist neocolonial conspiracy, bent on destroying him personally, as well as Iraq. It was a textbook example on how not manage a conflict.

The war that followed and its aftereffects denied convincingly the President's assertion that this was a "just war." To have been a "just war," it would have had to meet at least two key criteria: (1) the war should have been an act of last resort, after all efforts at a peaceful resolution had failed (which it was not, in view of the nearly total absence of direct negotiations between the two sides); and (2) the "good" achieved from the war should have outweighed its harmful effects (which it did not).   At a minimum, the war is responsible for the environmental disaster in the land, sea, and air around Kuwait; the damage to Kuwait's oil industry; and the unprecedented catastrophe that has befallen the Kurdish people of Iraq. It is also responsible for devastating much of the infrastructure of Iraq and Kuwait, each bearing war-related damage of as much as $100 billion. Iraq, according to U.N. findings, is also facing a "public health catastrophe," with thousands of Iraqi children expected to die from the aftereffects of the war and diseases caused by it.

The war is directly responsible for the death of perhaps as many as 100,000 Iraqi soldiers, plus unknown numbers of civilians. (Granted that Saddam's naked aggression started it all, did this absolve the United States of responsibility for killing more than 100,000 people to free 700,000 Kuwaitis?) To prosecute the war, the United States also spent upwards of $40 billion--this, amid the many unfunded problems at home dealing with education, public health, and the environment--and at least another $50 billion was contributed by its allies.[2]

Except for reversing the occupation of Kuwait, every issue on the Middle East's prewar agenda remains unfulfilled, despite the U.S. military victory. Hussein is still in power in Baghdad; thousands of

U.S. troops still remain in the area (with many more likely to return); plans for establishing a Gulf defense based on Arab forces are in shambles and so is the much heralded window of opportunity for settling the Arab-Israeli conflict; the Middle East governments are rearming themselves for the next war; and Kuwait, the city-state built on oil and in whose name this war was fought, continues to be the undemocratic political entity it has always been. The list of negatives resulting from the war goes on and on. The Gulf war may have been a military victory in that it forced the Iraqis out of Kuwait, but it was also an enormous U.S. moral defeat because of the thousands of unnecessary deaths and the destruction it has inflicted on Iraq and Kuwait.

"Was It Worth It?" asked *Time* in its August 5, 1991, issue, with the picture of Saddam on its cover and underneath the photo three reminders of some of the moral failures of the war: "The Mess in Kuwait; Saddam's Staying Power; A Rocky Road to Mideast Peace." The surprising answer that the majority of Americans give to this question is yes, although at a much lower level than in February 1991, when the war ended.[3] The answer says a great deal about American morality and also about the government's enormous ability to define issues and influence public opinion.

The war was worth it, assert its supporters. It liberated Kuwait, degraded Saddam's war machine, and shattered his influence and ability to threaten his neighbors. Had Hussein been allowed to go unchallenged, he would have been in control of over 40 percent of the world's oil reserves and would have used the revenue from this oil to build more and more powerful weapons to threaten our friends in the Gulf.[4] This judgment, of course, is extremely flawed. Saddam's aggression was never at issue with Americans, but the strategy and tactics that we used to accomplish our goal was. The Iraqi's actions were brutal and wrong, but so was the medicine that we handed him. We no longer live in an era when the use of arms is the only way for settling disputes. A real opportunity may have existed for settling this dispute peacefully, but the United States never bothered look for it.

In the aftermath of America's military victory, after the parades and celebrations have ended, we need to ask ourselves: Did winning the war make it right? Are we proud of what we accomplished in Kuwait, or will history record our involvement there as another exercise in gunboat diplomacy (the high-tech variety)? Is it possible that after defeating the Vietnam syndrome we will rush to embrace another syndrome, the one that says that we don't need to negotiate differences with other states, because we have the military power to overcome? Cases of naked aggression will surely arise in the future-- the world is full of Saddams. How will we react next time around? Will we again elect arms over diplomacy?

Great and powerful nations understand the limitations of their power and show great restraint. What happened in Iraq and Kuwait had nothing to do with what makes a nation great.[5]

NOTES

1. Elaine Sciolino, *The Outlaw State: Saddam Hussein's Quest for Power and the Gulf Crisis* (New York: Wiley, 1991), p. 16.

2. A U.S. General Accounting Office report, released in September 1991, estimates the total cost of Operation Desert Shield/Desert Storm to be over $100 billion.

3. According to a survey conducted by Americans Talk Issues, a respectable 62 percent still believe that the war was a great victory; this is a decline, however, of 22 percent from the 84 percent who thought so back in March 1991 (Americans Talk Issues, *The Emerging World Order*, Survey 16, June 23 to July 1, 1991, Winchester, MA).

4. Mortimer B. Zuckerman, "The Reasons to Celebrate," *U.S. News and World Report*, June 24, 1991.

5. Thomas C. Fox. *Iraq: Military Victory, Moral Defeat* (Kansas City: Sheed and Ward, 1991), p. 160.

Appendixes

A. U.N. RESOLUTIONS CONDEMNING IRAQ'S INVASION OF KUWAIT

Resolution 660 (August 2, 1990) condemned the invasion of Kuwait; demanded that Iraq immediately and unconditionally withdraw its forces to the positions held on August 1, 1990; called upon Iraq and Kuwait to begin negotiations for the resolution of their differences.

Resolution 661 (August 6, 1990) imposed a trade and financial embargo on Iraq and occupied Kuwait; called upon all member states to take appropriate measures to protect the assets of the legitimate government of Kuwait and not to recognize any regime set up in Kuwait by Iraq; established a committee (the Sanctions Committee) to monitor progress.

Resolution 662 (August 9, 1990) declared Iraq's annexation of Kuwait to be null and void; called upon all member states not to recognize the annexation.

Resolution 664 (August 18, 1990) demanded that Iraq permit the immediate departure from Kuwait and Iraq of the nationals of third countries and grant immediate and continuing access of consular officials to such nationals; demanded also that Iraq rescind its order closing diplomatic and consular missions in Kuwait.

Resolution 665 (August 25, 1990) called upon all member states with ships in the area to enforce the economic sanctions, by inspecting and verifying the cargoes and destinations of all incoming and outgoing shipping.

Resolution 666 (September 13, 1990) reaffirmed that Iraq remained fully responsible for the safety and well-being of foreign nationals in accordance with international humanitarian law, including the Fourth Geneva Convention.

Resolution 667 (September 16, 1990) condemned the aggressive acts perpetrated by Iraq against diplomatic premises and personnel in Kuwait, including the abduction of foreign nationals who were present in those premises; demanded the immediate release of all foreign nationals held in Iraq.

Resolution 669 (September 24, 1990) entrusted the Sanctions Committee with the responsibility for considering requests for assistance under the provisions of Article 50 of the Charter of the United Nations.

Resolution 670 (September 25, 1990) confirmed that Resolution 661 (1990) applied to all forms of transport, including aircraft; called upon all member states to detain ships of Iraq registry that were being or had been used to violate the economic embargo.

Resolution 671 (October 29, 1990) demanded that the Iraqi authorities cease and desist from taking hostages and mistreating and oppressing Kuwaiti and other foreign nationals; reminded Iraq that under international law it is liable for any loss, damage, or injury to Kuwait and other states as a result of its illegal invasion and occupation of Kuwait.

Resolution 677 (November 28, 1990) condemned the attempts by Iraq to alter the demographic composition of the population of Kuwait and to destroy the civil records maintained by the government of Kuwait.

Resolution 678 (November 29, 1990) authorized member states to use all necessary means to uphold and implement Security Council Resolution 660 (1990) and all subsequent relevant resolutions and to restore international peace and security in the area.

B. A STATEMENT BY U.S. CHURCH LEADERS, December 21, 1990

We are marching toward war. Indeed the stakes are horribly high. Military experts predict casualties in the tens and hundreds of thousands. And it won't end there. War would unleash a chain of human tragedies that will be with us for generations to come.

Our Christmas pilgrimage to the Middle East has utterly convinced us that war is not the answer. We believe the resort to massive violence to resolve the Gulf crisis would be politically and morally indefensible. . . . The unspeakable loss of lives, especially innocent civilians, would be unacceptable on moral grounds. Nations hold in their hands weapons of mass destruction. It is entirely possible that war in the Middle East will destroy everything. No cause will be served, no crisis resolved, no justice secured.

War will not liberate Kuwait, it will destroy it. War will not save us from weapons of mass destruction, it will unleash them. War will not establish regional stability, it will inflame the entire Middle East. . . .

While we do not accept the proposition that the resolution of all conflicts must precede the solution of the Gulf crisis, we do believe that there will be no lasting peace in the region until interrelated issues are dealt with in a comprehensive framework. What is required is not "linkage," but consistency in the implementation of U.S. foreign policy. Our government should support the convening of an international Middle East peace conference by the United Nations.

We have prayed in Jerusalem for the peace of Jerusalem. Jerusalem's vocation as the city of peace will not be realized until both Israelis and Palestinians are free and fully protected in the exercise of their human rights within secure and recognized boundaries.

We have seen both the hopes and the frustrations of Lebanon as it emerges from its 15-year nightmare of civil war. A durable peace in Lebanon requires the withdrawal of all foreign forces--Syrian, Israeli, and Iranian--and international support as Lebanon seeks to rebuild its shattered society.

We have felt the anguish of a divided Cyprus, which seems to have been forgotten by the world community. . . .

There is no such thing as a benign occupation. Occupation of the lands of others is wrong. It breeds frustration and frustration leads to conflict. Even as we oppose the Iraqi occupation of Kuwait on moral grounds, so also we believe that the West Bank and Gaza, Lebanon and Cyprus must be free. . . .

Having seen the face of the victims and potential victims, we believe that there must be an alternative to war. That alternative is negotiations--serious and substantive negotiations. . . . The United Nations can be the place where the deadly escalation of armaments of mass destruction in the Middle East can be reversed. . . . Our nation must not submit to the inevitability of war. . . .

C. THE JOINT CONGRESSIONAL RESOLUTION AUTHORIZING THE USE OF FORCE AGAINST IRAQ, January 12, 1991

WHEREAS the Government of Iraq without provocation invaded and occupied the territory of Kuwait on August 2, 1990; and

WHEREAS both the House of Representatives and the Senate have condemned Iraq's invasion of Kuwait and declared their support for international action to reverse Iraq's aggression; and

WHEREAS Iraq's conventional, chemical, biological and nuclear weapons and ballistic missile programs and its demonstrated willingness to use weapons of mass destruction pose a grave threat to world peace; and

WHEREAS the international community has demanded that Iraq withdraw unconditionally and immediately from Kuwait and that Kuwait's independence and legitimate government be restored; and . . .

WHEREAS in the absence of full compliance by Iraq with its resolutions, the U.N. Security Council in resolution 678 has authorized member states of the United Nations to use all necessary means, after January 15, 1991, to uphold and implement all relevant Security Council resolutions and to restore international peace and security in the area; . . .

The President is authorized . . . to use U.S. armed forces pursuant to U.N. Security Council Resolution 678 (1990) in order to achieve implementation of Security Council Resolutions 660, 661, 662, 664, 665, 666, 667, 669, 670, 674 and 677.

Before exercising the authority granted (above) the President shall make available to the Speaker of the House of Representatives and the President *pro tempore* of the Senate his determination that:

(1) the United States has used all appropriate diplomatic and other peaceful means to obtain compliance by Iraq with the U.N. Security Council resolutions cited . . . and

(2) that those efforts have not been and would not be successful in obtaining such compliance.

D. THE PRESIDENT'S LETTER TO THE CONGRESS, January 16, 1991

I have concluded that:

1. The United States has used all appropriate diplomatic and other peaceful means to obtain compliance by Iraq with U.N. Security Council Resolutions 660, 661, 662, 664, 665, 666, 667, 669, 670, 677, and 678; and

2. These efforts have not been and would not be successful in obtaining such compliance.

Background. For over five and a half months, the international community has sought with unprecedented unity to reverse Iraq's brutal and unprovoked aggression against Kuwait. The United States and the vast majority of governments of the world, working together through the United Nations, have been united both in their determination to compel Iraq's withdrawal from Kuwait and in their strong preference for doing so through peaceful means. Since August 2, we have sought to build maximum diplomatic and economic pressure against Iraq. Regrettably, Iraq has given no sign whatever that it intends to comply with the will of the international community; nor is there any indication that diplomatic and economic means alone would ever compel Iraq to do so . . . .

From the beginning of the Gulf crisis, the United States has consistently pursued four basic objectives: (1) the immediate, complete, and unconditional Iraqi withdrawal from Kuwait; (2) the restoration of the legitimate Government of Kuwait; (3) the protection of U.S. citizens abroad;

and (4) the security and stability of a region vital to U.S. national security. In pursuit of these objectives, we have sought and obtained action by the U.N. Security Council, resulting in twelve separate resolutions that have been fully consistent with U.S. objectives. . . .

U.N. Security Council Resolution 678 of 29 November 1990, authorizes U.N. member states to use "all necessary means" to implement Resolution 660 and all subsequent relevant resolutions of the Security Council, and to restore international peace and security in the area, unless Iraq fully implements those resolutions on or before January 15, 1991. . . .

Iraq has taken no steps whatever to fulfill these requirements. Iraq has forcefully stated that it considers the Security Council's resolutions invalid and has no intention of complying with them at any time. Iraqi forces remain in occupation of Kuwait and have been substantially reinforced in recent weeks rather than withdrawn. Iraq has strongly and repeatedly reiterated its annexation of Kuwait and stated its determination that Kuwait will remain permanently a part of Iraq. . . .

In short, the government of Iraq remains completely intransigent in rejecting the U.N. Security Council's demands--despite the exhaustive use by the United States and the United Nations of all appropriate diplomatic, political, and economic measures to persuade or compel Iraq to comply. . . .

The extensive diplomatic and political efforts undertaken by the United States . . . to persuade or compel Iraq to withdraw from Kuwait have not succeeded. The U.N. Security Council and General Assembly have overwhelmingly and repeatedly condemned the Iraqi invasion and demanded Iraq's immediate and unconditional withdrawal from Kuwait. The Security Council has invoked its extraordinary authority under Chapter VII of the U.N. Charter, not only to order comprehensive economic sanctions, but to authorize the use of all other means necessary, including the use of force. . . .

The President, the Secretary of State and other U.S. officials have engaged in an exhaustive process of consultation with other governments and international organizations. The Secretary of State alone has . . . traveled over 125,000 miles in the course of these contacts. . . . This extensive diplomacy . . . has not caused the government of Iraq to withdraw from Kuwait.

More recently, on January 9, the Secretary of State met at length in Geneva with the Iraqi Foreign Minister, who in six and one-half hours of talks demonstrated no readiness whatever to implement the U.N. Security Council resolutions. The Iraqi Foreign Minister even refused to receive a diplomatic communication from the President intended for Saddam Hussein. . . . For our part, the administration made clear that there could be no reward for aggression. . . . Attempts to link resolution of Iraq's aggression against Kuwait with other issues were rejected on the grounds that these issues were unrelated to Iraq's aggression. . . .

E. THE U.S.-SOVIET JOINT STATEMENT, January 29, 1991

(Issued in Washington, D.C., at the conclusion of discussions between U.S. Secretary of State James Baker and then-Soviet Foreign Minister Alexander Bessmertnykh)

The ministers reiterated the commitment of their countries to the U.N. Security Council resolutions adopted in connection with Iraq's aggression against Kuwait. . . . The military actions authorized by the United Nations have been provoked by the refusal of the Iraqi leadership to comply with the clear and lawful demands of the international community for withdrawal from Kuwait.

Secretary Baker emphasized that the United States and its coalition partners are seeking the liberation of Kuwait, not the destruction of Iraq. He stressed that the United States has no quarrel with the people of Iraq, and poses no threat to Iraq's territorial integrity. Secretary Baker reiterated that the United States is doing its utmost to avoid casualties among the civilian population and is not interested in expanding the conflict.

Minister of Foreign Affairs Bessmertnykh . . . agreed that Iraq's withdrawal from Kuwait must remain the goal of the international community. Both sides believe that everything possible should be done to avoid further escalation of the war and expansion of its scale.

The ministers continue to believe that a cessation of hostilities would be possible if Iraq would make an unequivocal commitment to withdraw from Kuwait. They also believe that such a commitment must be backed by immediate concrete steps leading to full compliance with the Security Council resolutions. . . .

The ministers agreed that establishing enduring stability and peace in the region after the conflict, on the basis of effective security arrangements, will be high priority of our two governments. . . .

In addition, dealing with the causes of instability and the sources of conflict, including the Arab-Israeli conflict, will be especially important. Indeed both ministers agreed that without a meaningful peace process--one which promotes a just peace, security, and real reconciliation for Israel, Arab states and Palestinians--it will not be possible to deal with the sources of conflict and instability in the region. Both ministers, therefore, agreed that in the aftermath of the crisis in the Persian Gulf, mutual U.S./Soviet efforts to promote Arab-Israeli peace and regional stability . . . will be greatly facilitated and enhanced. . .

F. STATEMENT BY THE IRAQI REVOLUTIONARY COMMAND COUNCIL, February 15, 1991

The Revolutionary Command Council declares the following:

First, Iraq is ready to deal with Security Council Resolution 660 of 1990, with the aim of reaching an honorable and acceptable political solution, including withdrawal. The Iraqi pledge is linked to the following:

a) A total and comprehensive cease-fire on land, air, and sea.

b) Cancellation by the Security Council of resolutions 661, 662, 664, 665, 666, 669, 670, 674, 677, and 678 and of their provisions, including the cancellation of all measures of boycott and embargo directed against Iraq.

c) The United States and other countries participating in the aggression against Iraq to withdraw all their forces, weapons and equipment from the Middle East, including the weapons and equipment provided to Israel under the pretext of the crisis in the Gulf.

d) Israel to withdraw from Palestine and the Arab territories it is occupying in the Golan and southern Lebanon. If Israel fails to do this, the United Nations should then enforce against Israel the same sanctions it has enacted against Iraq.

e) Iraq's historical rights on land and at sea should be guaranteed in full in any peaceful solution.

f) The political arrangements for Kuwait should proceed from the people's will, and in accordance with a genuine democratic practice, and not on the basis of the rights acquired by the Sabah family.

Second, the countries that have participated in the aggression undertake to reconstruct what the aggression has destroyed in Iraq. Iraq should not incur any financial burdens in this regard.

Third, the debts of Iraq and of other countries in the region which were harmed by the aggression should be written off.

Fourth, the Gulf states, including Iran, should be given the task of freely drawing up security arrangements in the region and of organizing relations among them without foreign interference.

Fifth, the Arabian Gulf region should be declared a zone free of foreign military bases.

G. THE PRESIDENT'S RESPONSE, February 15, 1991

When I first heard that statement, I must say I was happy that Saddam Hussein had seemed to realize that he must now withdraw unconditionally from Kuwait. . . . Regrettably, the Iraq statement now appears to be a cruel hoax, dashing the hopes of the people of Iraq and, indeed around the world. . . .

Not only was the Iraq statement full of unacceptable old conditions, but Saddam Hussein has added several new conditions. . .   Now let me state once again: they must withdraw without condition and there must be full implementation of all Security Council resolutions. And there will be no linkage to other problems in the area, and the legitimate rulers of Kuwait must be returned to Kuwait.

Until a massive withdrawal begins, with those Iraqi troops visibly leaving Kuwait, the coalition forces . . . will continue their efforts to force compliance with all resolutions of the United Nations.

But there's another way for the bloodshed to stop, and that is for the Iraqi military and the Iraqi people to take matters into their own hands, to force Saddam Hussein the dictator to step aside and to comply with the United Nations resolutions and then rejoin the family of peace-loving nations. . . .

H. THE SOVIET PEACE PROPOSAL, February 22, 1991

An official spokesman for Soviet President Gorbachev announced on February 22, 1991, Iraqi acceptance of the following terms for ending the Gulf war:

1. Iraq to carry out Resolution 660 of the U.N. Security Council, i.e., withdraw its forces immediately and unconditionally from Kuwait. The troop withdrawal will begin the day after a cease-fire is agreed upon, and be completed within 21 days. Troop withdrawal from Kuwait City will be accomplished within the first four days.

2. Once the Iraqi troops have withdrawn from Kuwait, all U.N. Security Council resolutions against Iraq will be lifted as no longer applicable.

3. All prisoners of war will be freed and repatriated within three days of the cease-fire.

4. The cease-fire and withdrawal of Iraqi troops from Kuwait will be monitored by U.N. designated peacekeeping forces.

I. THE PRESIDENT'S ULTIMATUM, February 22, 1991

In view of the Soviet initiative, which very frankly we appreciate, we want to set forth this morning the specific criteria that will insure Saddam Hussein complies with the United Nations mandate. . . .

We learned this morning that Saddam has now launched a scorched-earth policy against Kuwait, anticipating perhaps that he will now be forced to leave. He is wantonly setting fires to and destroying the oil wells, the oil tanks, the port terminals and other installations of that small country.

Indeed, they are destroying the entire oil-production system of Kuwait. And at the same time that the Moscow press conference was going on and Iraq's Foreign Minister was talking peace, Saddam Hussein was launching Scud missiles. . . .

The coalition will give Saddam Hussein until noon Saturday to do what he must do--begin his immediate and unconditional withdrawal from Kuwait. We must hear publicly and authoritatively his acceptance of these terms. . . .

(The "terms" referred to by the President were included in a statement read by Marlin Fitzwater, the President's spokesman:

. . . The United States, after consulting with the government of Kuwait and our other coalition partners, declares that a ground campaign will not be initiated against Iraqi forces if prior to noon Saturday, February 23, New York time, Iraq publicly accepts the following terms:

1. Iraq must begin large-scale withdrawal from Kuwait by noon New York time, Saturday, February 23 and complete military withdrawal from Kuwait in one week. Kuwait City is to be freed within the first 48 hours so as to allow the prompt return of the legitimate government of Kuwait. Within the one week specified above, Iraq must return all its forces to their positions of August 1 in accordance with Resolution 660.

2. In cooperation with the International Red Cross, Iraq must release all prisoners of war and third-country civilians being held against their will and return the remains of killed and deceased servicemen.

3. Iraq must remove all explosives or booby traps, including those on Kuwaiti oil installations, and provide data on the location and nature of any land or sea mines.

4. Iraq must cease combat air fire, aircraft flights over Iraq and Kuwait, except for transport aircraft carrying troops out of Kuwait. It must cease all destructive actions against Kuwaiti citizens and property and release all Kuwaiti detainees.)

J. THE PRESIDENT'S ADDRESS BEFORE A JOINT SESSION OF THE CONGRESS, March 6, 1991

From the moment Operation Desert Storm commenced on January 16 until the time the guns fell silent at midnight one week ago, this nation has watched its sons and daughters with pride--watched over them with prayer. As Commander in Chief, I can report to you that our armed forces fought with honor and valor. And as President, I can report to the nation that aggression is defeated. The war is over.

This is a victory for every nation in the coalition; for the United Nations; a victory for unprecedented international cooperation. . . . It is a victory for the rule of law and for what is right. . . .

The recent challenge could not have been clearer. Saddam Hussein was the villain; Kuwait the victim. To the aid of this small country came the nations of North America and Europe, from Asia and South America, from Africa and the Arab world. . . . Tonight in Iraq, Saddam walks amidst ruin. His war machine is crushed. The ability to threaten mass destruction is itself destroyed. . . . And when his defeated legions come home, all Iraqis will see and feel the havoc he has wrought. For all that Saddam has done to his own people, to the Kuwaitis, and to the entire world, Saddam and those around him are accountable. . . .

Our commitment to peace in the Middle East does not end with the liberation of Kuwait. So tonight, let me outline four key challenges to be met.

First, we must work together to create shared security arrangements in the region. Our friends and allies in the Middle East recognize that they will bear the bulk of this responsibility for regional security. But we want them to know that just as we stood with them to repel aggression, so now America stands ready to work with them to secure peace. This does not mean stationing ground forces on the Arabian peninsula, but it does mean American participation in joint exercises involving air and ground forces. It means maintaining a capable U.S. naval presence in the region just as we have for over 40 years. Let it be clear: our vital national interests depend on a stable and secure Gulf.

Second, we must act to control the proliferation of weapons of mass destruction and the missiles used to deliver them. It would be tragic if the nations of the Middle East and Persian Gulf were now, in the wake of the war, to embark on a new arms race. . . .

Third, we must work to create new opportunities for peace and stability in the Middle East. . . . Security does not come from military power alone. All of us know the depth of bitterness that has made the dispute between Israel and its neighbors so painful and intractable. Yet, in the conflict just concluded, Israel and many Arab states have, for the first time, found themselves confronting the same aggressor. By now, it should be plain to all parties that peacemaking in the Middle East requires compromise. . . . We must do all that we can to close the gap between Israel and the Arab states and between Israelis and Palestinians. . . .

Fourth, we must foster economic development for the sake of peace and progress. The Persian Gulf and Middle East form a region rich in natural resources with a wealth of untapped human potential. Resources once squandered on military might must be redirected to more peaceful ends. . . .

K. THE U.N. REPORT ON HUMANITARIAN NEEDS OF IRAQ, March 20, 1991

(Prepared by Under Secretary General M. Ahtisaari)

Nothing that we had seen or read had quite prepared us for the particular form of devastation which has now befallen the country. The recent conflict has wrought near-apocalyptic results upon the economic infrastructure of what had been, until January 1991, a rather highly urbanized and mechanized society. Now, most means of modern life support have been destroyed or rendered tenuous. Iraq has, for some time to come, been relegated to a pre-industrial age, but with all the disabilities of post-industrial dependency on an intensive use of energy and technology. . . .

As a result of war, virtually all previously viable sources of fuel and power and modern means of communication are now, essentially, defunct. The far-reaching implications of this energy and communications vacuum as regards urgent humanitarian support are of crucial significance for the nature and effectiveness of the international response. . . .

The authorities are as yet scarcely able to even measure the dimensions of the calamity, much less respond to its consequences, because they cannot obtain full and accurate data. Additionally, there is much less than the minimum fuel required to provide the energy needed for movement or transportation, irrigation or generators for power to pump water and sewage. For instance, emergency medical supplies can be moved to health centers only with extreme difficulty, and usually, major delay. . . . Most employees are simply unable to come to work. Both the authorities and the trade unions estimate that approximately 90 percent of industrial workers have been reduced to inactivity and will be deprived of income as of the end of March. . . .

All evidence indicates that flour is now at a critically low level, and that supplies of sugar, rice, tea, vegetable oil, powdered milk, and pulses are currently at critically low levels or have been exhausted. . . . This year's grain harvest in June is seriously compromised for a number of reasons, including failure of irrigation/drainage (no power for pumps, lack of spare parts); lack of pesticides and fertilizers (previously imported); and lack of fuel and spare parts for the highly-mechanized and fuel-dependent harvesting machines. Should this harvest fail, or be below average, as is very likely barring a rapid change in the situation, widespread starvation conditions become a real possibility. . . .

There needs to be a major mobilization and movement of resources to deal with aspects of this deep crisis in the fields of agriculture and food, water, sanitation and health. . . . It will be difficult, if not impossible, to remedy these immediate humanitarian needs without dealing with the underlying need for energy, on an equally urgent basis. The need for energy means, initially, emergency oil imports and the rapid patching up of a limited refining and electricity production capacity with essential supplies from other countries. Otherwise, food that is imported cannot be preserved and distributed; water cannot be purified; sewage cannot be pumped away and cleansed; crops cannot be irrigated, medicaments cannot be conveyed where they are required; needs cannot even be effectively assessed. It is unmistakable that the Iraqi people may soon face a further imminent catastrophe, which could include epidemic and famine, if massive life-supporting needs are not rapidly met. The long summer, with its often 45 or 50 degrees temperatures (113-122 degrees F) is only weeks away. Time is short.

L. THE U.N. CEASE-FIRE RESOLUTION, April 3, 1991 (Resolution 687)

1. Demands that Iraq and Kuwait respect the inviolability of the international boundary established in the October 4, 1963, treaty between the two nations.

2. Requests the Secretary-General to submit a plan for the immediate deployment of a U.N. observer unit to monitor the Khor Abdullah and a demilitarized zone extending 10 kilometers into Iraq and 5 kilometers into Kuwait.

3. Invites Iraq to reaffirm unconditionally its obligations under the Geneva Protocol of 1925 and of the Biological Weapons Convention of 1972.

4. Decides that Iraq shall unconditionally accept the destruction under international supervision of all chemical and biological weapons, of their research and manufacturing facilities, and of all ballistic missiles with a range greater than 150 kilometers.

5. Directs that Iraq submit to the Secretary-General a declaration on the location, amounts and types of all weapons in paragraph 4 above and to agree to their on-site inspection by U.N. representatives.

6. Forbids Iraq from using, developing, constructing or acquiring the weapons referred to in paragraph 4, above, and requests the Secretary General to develop a plan for the monitoring and verification of Iraq's compliance with this requirement.

7. Invites Iraq to reaffirm its obligations under the Treaty on the Non-Proliferation of Nuclear Weapons of July 1, 1968.

8. Decides that Iraq shall unconditionally agree not to acquire or develop nuclear weapons or subsystems thereof, and to submit to the U.N. Secretary-General a declaration on the locations, amounts and types of nuclear materials under its possession.

9. Requests the Director-General of the International Atomic Energy

Agency to carry out on-site inspection of Iraq's nuclear capabilities and to develop a plan for their removal, destruction or rendering harmless.

10. Requests the Secretary-General to facilitate the return of all Kuwaiti property seized by Iraq.

11. Reaffirms that Iraq is liable under international law for any direct loss, damage, including environmental damage and the deletion of natural resources, as a result of its unlawful invasion and occupation of Kuwait.

12. Demands that Iraq adhere scrupulously to all its obligations concerning servicing and repayment of its foreign debt.

13. Creates a fund to meet the requirement for payment of the claims established in paragraph 11, above. The fund is to be financed from a percentage of profits from Iraq's petroleum exports.

14. Lifts the prohibition against the sale of foodstuffs to Iraq.

15. Reaffirms the continuation of sanctions against the sale or supply to Iraq of arms and related materiel of all types.

16. Directs Iraq to assist the International Committee of the Red Cross in its search for missing Kuwaitis and other victims of the war.

17. Requires Iraq to renounce terrorism, to end support to acts of international terrorism, and to prohibit terrorist organizations from operating within its territory.

Chronology

August 2, 1990 Iraq invades Kuwait. The U.N. Security Council condemns the invasion.

August 6, 1990 The U.N. Security Council imposes worldwide economic sanctions on Iraq. The President orders air and ground forces to the Gulf.

August 8, 1990 Iraq annexes Kuwait.

August 12, 1990 Saddam Hussein links the Kuwait crisis with the Israeli occupation of Arab lands.

August 25, 1990 The U.N. Security Council calls upon its members to enforce the sanctions.

August 28, 1990 Iraq refuses to withdraw from Kuwait and declares it to be its nineteenth province.

September 9, 1990 Presidents Bush and Gorbachev meet in Helsinki and condemn the invasion of Kuwait and demand Iraqi withdrawal.

November 8, 1990 President Bush orders 200,000 additional forces to the Persian Gulf to give the U.S. commander in the area an "offensive option."

November 29, 1990 The U.N. Security Council establishes a deadline of January 15, 1991, for Iraq's evacuation of Kuwait and enacts a resolution approving the use of "all necessary means" for that purpose.

November 30, 1990 President Bush offers to meet Iraqi Foreign Minister

Aziz and proposes to send Secretary Baker to Baghdad to talk with Saddam Hussein.

December 6, 1990 Saddam announces that all foreign hostages are free to leave Iraq.

January 9, 1991 A meeting between Iraqi Foreign Minister Aziz and U.S. Secretary of State Baker in Geneva ends in a deadlock.

January 12, 1991 Both houses of the Congress approve the use of force to free Kuwait.

January 15, 1991 U.N.-imposed deadline passes. Iraqi forces are still in Kuwait.

January 17, 1991 (January 16, 6:30 p.m. EST) President Bush orders U.S. and allied aircraft to strike targets in Iraq and Kuwait. Hundreds of aircraft and Tomahawk cruise missiles participate in the attack. Targets being struck include missile launching sites, airfields, telecommunication centers, air defense facilities, and nuclear, biological, and chemical facilities.

January 18, 1991 Air raids against targets in Iraq and Kuwait are continuing. At 2 a.m. local time, eight conventionally armed Scud missiles strike Haifa and Tel Aviv, but another Scud fired at Dhahran is intercepted by a Patriot antimissile missile.

January 19, 1991 U.S. and allied raids are continuing from bases in Dhahran, Oman, Qatar, and Turkey and from aircraft carriers in the Red Sea and the Persian Gulf. Virtually all of Iraq's nuclear, chemical, and biological weapons facilities reportedly have been destroyed.

January 20, 1991 Scuds again attack Israeli and Saudi cities. U.S. air defense units armed with Patriot antimissile missiles arrive in Israel. Allied prisoners are interviewed on Iraqi television.

January 21, 1991 Iraq reportedly is using U.S. and allied prisoners of war as human shields at key military and industrial sites. The United States is denouncing the action as a violation of the Geneva Conventions.

January 22, 1991 A Scud missile explodes in a Tel Aviv neighborhood, causing numerous casualties. Improved weather allows resumption of large-scale bombing against targets in Iraq and Kuwait, raising the total of missions flown to 10,000. Iraq starts a scorched-earth policy: sets fire to

Kuwaiti oil wells and storage tanks and pumps huge amounts of crude oil into the Gulf.

January 23, 1991 U.S. and allied air raids are shifting emphasis to targets in area of Basra, where Republican Guard troops are dug in. The Iraqi air force continues to abstain from fighting; fewer than 20 Iraqi planes have been encountered to date, out of an inventory of over 700.

January 25, 1991 The United States is charging that Iraq is sabotaging a Kuwaiti supertanker terminal, dumping millions of barrels of oil into the Persian Gulf.

January 26, 1991 About 20 Iraqi aircraft flee to Iran, in an apparent effort to survive intensified U.S. air raids at Iraqi airfields. The oil spill off Kuwait is growing; it threatens Saudi desalination plants. The U.S. air campaign is continuing; so are Iraqi Scud attacks on Israel and Saudi Arabia.

January 27, 1991 Missions flown since the beginning of the air campaign total 22,000, averaging about 2,000 per day. Twenty additional Iraqi aircraft seek refuge in Iran.

January 29, 1991 Fifty more Iraqi planes escape to Iran. The U.N. Secretary General receives assurances from Iran that the aircraft will not be returned until after the war. Around-the-clock bombing of targets in Iraq and Kuwait continues.

January 30, 1991 Iraqi troops and armor push into Saudi Arabia and occupy the town of Khafji, touching off the first ground battle of the war. Iraqi war planes continue to escape to Iran (with at least 100 aircraft already there). The Pentagon announces that the entire Iraqi navy has been destroyed.

January 31, 1991 U.S. Marines and Saudi and Qatari forces retake Khafji after intense ground combat. Hundreds of Iraqis are taken prisoner. Iraqi aircraft now in Iran total 120, including F-1 Mirages, MIG-29s, and SU-24s.

February 3, 1991 Total missions flown since the beginning of the war reach 44,000. The battleships *Missouri* and *Wisconsin* begin artillery shelling of dug-in Iraqi Republican Guards. President Rafsanjani of Iran offers to mediate peaceful settlement between the United States and Iraq. The U.S. government reacts coolly to the offer.

February 5, 1991 Iraq reports that 428 civilians were killed and 650 wounded since the beginning of the air campaign.

February 6, 1991 Iraq continues to report civilian losses due to U.S. and allied air raids and claims that 150 persons were killed in the raid on Nasiriyah; 350, in the bombings of Basra.

February 7, 1991 Total missions flown since the beginning of the war reach more than 52,000. Additional Iraqi aircraft flee to Iran, increasing the total there to 135. U.S. and allied forces in the Gulf now total about 705,000; Iraqi strength in the Kuwait theater of operations is estimated at 545,000, including about 150,000 Republican Guards.

February 9, 1991 U.S. military authorities report that about 20 percent of Iraq's armor and artillery have been destroyed as a result of the air war, including 750 tanks, 600 armored personnel carriers, and 650 artillery pieces. The frequency of Scud attacks on Israel and Saudi Arabia is declining. Thirty Scuds have been fired to date against Israel; 28, against Saudi Arabia.

February 10, 1991 Secretary of Defense Cheney and General Powell meet with U.S. and allied field commanders to evaluate their readiness for a ground assault. The air campaign is accelerating. The number of air missions flown to date is nearing 60,000.

February 11, 1991 Soviet envoy Yevgeni Primakov arrives in Baghdad in a last-ditch effort to negotiate peace between the allies and Iraq. U.S. and allied ground artillery and naval gunfire are "preparing" southern Kuwait for the expected ground attack.

February 13, 1991 A U.S. aircraft drops two bombs on a reinforced concrete building in Baghdad, killing hundreds of civilians. Iraq claims the building was a civilian air-raid shelter. U.S. military authorities assert it was a military command and control center.

February 14, 1991 The U.S. bombardment of Iraqi positions in Kuwait is reaching cataclysmic proportions. About a third of Iraq's tanks and artillery are already destroyed. Nearly 70,000 air sorties have been flown since the beginning of the war. The air-raid shelter/bunker controversy continues, as Iraqis remove additional dead from the building.

February 15, 1991 Saddam Hussein offers to withdraw his troops from Kuwait but imposes several conditions. President Bush dismisses the offer as a "hoax." It has no effect on the war. Air strikes on Iraqi targets are continuing. U.S. and allied ground forces reportedly are on the move. A land offensive is imminent.

February 16, 1991 U.S. and allied troops are continuing major redeployment along the Saudi-Iraq-Kuwait border in preparation for a ground war.

February 17, 1991 Iraqi Foreign Minister Aziz meets President Gorbachev in Moscow and receives from him a plan for the political settlement of the war. In the air war, the number of sorties flown reaches 80,000. The U.S. destroyer *Princeton* and helicopter carrier *Tripoli* are damaged by Iraqi mines.

February 19, 1991 Air pounding of Iraqi forces continues, with Baghdad also struck. An Iraqi official claims that casualties to date exceed 20,000 dead and 60,000 wounded, both civilian and military. President Bush says the Soviet plan falls short.

February 21, 1991 Iraqi Foreign Minister Aziz returns to Moscow and again meets President Gorbachev. A Soviet spokesman announces that Iraq has replied positively to President Gorbachev's proposal based on a full and unconditional Iraqi withdrawal from Kuwait. President Bush expresses serious concerns with the plan. Heavy air bombardment and artillery barrage continue as a prelude to full-scale ground war. Air sorties to date total 88,000.

February 22, 1991 President Bush issues an ultimatum, allowing Iraq one week to withdraw from Kuwait or face an allied ground attack. Withdrawal must begin by noon on February 23. Opposing forces consist of 532,000 U.S. troops, 205,000 coalition troops, and 545,000 Iraqis (in the Kuwait theater of operations). The air war and preparations for a ground offensive continue.

February 23, 1991 President Bush orders the start of the ground war. U.S. and allied forces invade Kuwait. Large numbers of Iraqi troops are surrendering. In Kuwait, retreating Iraqis are taking hostages, executing civilians, and setting oil installations on fire.

February 24, 1991 U.S. and allied troops drive deep into Kuwait and surround Kuwait City. In the west, large, more powerful forces are executing a wide flanking maneuver designed to entrap the entire Iraqi army south of Basra. Allied troops meet only sporadic resistance. Thousands of Iraqis are surrendering.

February 25, 1991 A Scud missile lands in a Dhahran barracks housing American troops; 28 service persons are killed in the most devastating attack yet. An allied flanking maneuver is completed as U.S. and allied troops reach the Euphrates River. The Iraqi army is encircled and in full retreat. Thousands of prisoners are taken. Baghdad radio announces that Saddam Hussein has ordered his army out of Kuwait. The U.S. government dismisses the move as not sufficient to end the war.

February 26, 1991 Iraqi army is in full retreat but unable to escape across the Euphrates River. Thousands of trapped and retreating Iraqis are killed by superior U.S. armor and pounding from the air. Arab forces enter Kuwait City.

February 27, 1991 President Bush orders a cease-fire. All fighting ends. Iraqis are beaten and driven out of Kuwait in less than 100 hours. Eighty thousand prisoners are taken.

March 2, 1991 U.S. officials report fighting in Basra between retreating Republican Guards and Shiite rebels.

March 3, 1991 U.S. field commanders meet with their Iraqi counterparts in Safwan, Iraq, and agree on the terms of a cease-fire.

March 4, 1991 The Shiite rebellion in southern Iraq is gaining momentum. Kurds, in the north, also rise against Saddam's regime.

March 7, 1991 Shiite and Kurdish rebellions are spreading but are meeting stiff resistance from Republican Guards. Intense fighting is reported in several populated centers.

March 13, 1991 Kurdish leaders report that their forces now control 75 percent of northern Iraq, but charge that Iraqis are using helicopters to suppress them.   President Bush warns Iraq against the use of helicopters to combat opponents of the regime.

March 14, 1991 The Emir of Kuwait returns to Kuwait City.

March 16, 1991 Saddam Hussein announces that the revolt in southern Iraq has been crushed.

March 20, 1991 A U.S. F-15 shoots down an Iraqi fighter-bomber for violating the terms of the cease-fire.

March 22, 1991 The U.N. Security Council lifts the embargo on food supplies to Iraq and on certain critical humanitarian goods.

March 23, 1991 A U.S. F-15 shoots another Iraqi fighter-bomber for violating the ban on flying.

March 26, 1991 The U.S. government officially announces that it is not taking a position in Iraq's civil war.

March 28, 1991 Fighting continues in the north, especially for the control of the oil city of Kirkuk.

April 3, 1991 The U.N. Security Council votes a cease-fire resolution for ending the war.

April 4, 1991 The Kurdish rebellion collapses. Hundreds of thousands of Kurds flee toward Iran and Turkey.

April 7, 1991 U.S. aircraft begin delivering humanitarian aid to Kurdish refugees.

April 11, 1991 Iraq accepts the terms of the cease-fire resolution; the U.N. Security Council formally declares the end of the war.

April 16, 1991 President Bush orders the U.S. military to establish encampments in northern Iraq to shelter the Kurdish refugees.

May 29, 1991 President Bush announces a series of proposals intended to curb the spread of nuclear, chemical, and biological weapons in the Middle East, as well as the missiles that can deliver them.

June 3, 1991 The Emir of Kuwait announces that parliamentary elections in his nation will be held in October 1992.

Additional Reading

BOOKS

Allen, Thomas F., et al. *CNN Reports: War in the Gulf*. Atlanta: Turner Publishing, 1991.

Blackwell, James. *Thunder in the Desert: The Strategies and Tactics of the Persian Gulf War*. New York: Bantam Books, 1991.

Brenner, Eliot, and William Harwood. *Desert Storm: The Weapons of War*. New York: Orion Books, 1991.

Chadwick, Frank, and Matt Caffrey. *Gulf War Fact Book*. GDW,1991.

Cohen, Roger, and Claudio Gatti. *In the Eye of the Storm: The Life of General H. Norman Schwarzkopf*. New York: Farrar, Straus and Giroux, 1991.

Cordesman, Anthony H. *Weapons of Mass Destruction in the Middel East: A Royal United Services Institute Study*. London: Brasseys'(UK), 1991.

David, Peter. *Triumph in the Desert: The Challenge, the Fighting, the Legacy*. New York: Random House, 1991.

Fox, Thomas C. *Iraq: Military Victory, Moral Defeat*. Kansas City: Sheed and Ward, 1991.

Friedman, Norman. *Desert Victory: The War for Kuwait*. Annapolis, MD:Naval Institute Press, 1991.

Henderson, Simon. *Instant Empire: Saddam Hussein's Ambition for Iraq*. San Francisco: Mercury House, 1991.

Karsh, Efraim, and Inari Rautsi. *Saddam Hussein: A Political Biography*. New York: Free Press, 1991.

al-Khalil, Samir. *Republic of Fear: The Inside Story of Saddam's Iraq*. New York: Pantheon, 1990.

Miller, Judith, and Laurie Mylroie. *Saddam Hussein and the Crisis in the Gulf*. New York: Time Books/Random House, 1990.

Nolan, Janne E. *Trappings of Power: Ballistic Missiles in the Third World*. Washington, D.C.: Brookings Institution, 1991.

Salinger, Pierre, and Eric Laurent. *Secret Dossier: The Hidden Agenda Behind the Gulf War*. New York: Penguin, 1991.

Sasson, Jean P. *The Rape of Kuwait*. Los Angeles: Knightsbridge, 1991.

Sciolino, Elaine. *The Outlaw State: Saddam Hussein's Quest for Power and the Gulf Crisis*. New York: Wiley, 1991.

Sifry, Mical L, and Christopher Cerf, eds. *The Gulf War Reader*. New York: Times Books, 1991.

Spector, Leonard S., with Jacqueline R. Smith. *Nuclear Ambitions*. Boulder, Colo: Westview Press, 1990.

Time. Desert Storm: The War in the Persian Gulf. New York: Time Books, 1991.

Vogt, William M. et.al. *Desert Storm*. Leesburg, VA: Empire Press, 1991.

Wiener, Robert. *Live from Baghdad: Gathering News at Ground Zero*. New York: Doubleday, 1991.

Woodward, Bob. *The Commanders*. New York: Simon and Schuster, 1991.

ARTICLES

Albright, David, and Mark Hibbs. "Iraq's Nuclear Hide and Seek," *Bulletin of the Atomic Scientists*, September 1991 and "Iraq's Bomb: Blueprints and Artifacts," *Bulletin of the Atomic Scientists*, January\February 1992.

Cohen, Avner, and Marvin Miller. "Iraq and the Rules of the Nuclear Game," *Bulletin of the Atomic Scientists*, July/August 1991.

Fotion, Nicholas G. "The Gulf War: Cleanly Fought," *Bulletin of the Atomic Scientists*, September 1991.

Fuller, Graham E. "Moscow and the Gulf War," *Foreign Affairs*, Summer 1991.

Hamilton, Lee H. "Middle Eastern Arms Restraint: An Obligation to

Act," *Arms Control Today*, June 1991.

Leonard, James. "Steps Toward a Middle East Free of Nuclear Weapons," *Arms Control Today*, April 1991.

Lopez, George A. "The Gulf War: Not So Clean," *Bulletin of the Atomic Scientists*, September 1991.

Oberdorfer, Don. "Missed Signals in the Middle East," *Washington Post Magazine*, March 17, 1991.

Pardew, James W. Jr., "The Iraqi Army's Defeat in Kuwait," *Parameters*, Winter 1991-92.

Pipes, Daniel. "Is Damascus Ready for Peace?" *Foreign Affairs*, Fall 1991.

Primakov, Yevgeni. "The Inside Story of Moscow's Quest for a Deal," *Time*, March 4, 1991.

-----. "My Final Visit with Saddam Hussein," *Time*, March 11, 1991.

Roberts, Brad. "Iraq's Chemical Weapons as Overrated as Scuds," *Wall Street Journal*, February 8, 1991.

Smith, Jeffrey R. "Iraq's Secret A-Arms Effort: Grim Lessons for the World," *Washington Post*, Outlook Section, August 11, 1991.

Steinbruner, John D. "The Consequences of the Gulf War," *Brookings Review*, Spring 1991.

Stewart, Thomas A. "Winning the Peace," *Fortune*, February 25, 1991.

Williams, Pete. "The Press and the Persian Gulf War," *Parameters*, August 1991.

OTHER PUBLICATIONS

Americans Talk Issues. *The New World Order--What the Peace Should Be*. Survey No. 15. Winchester, MA, March 1991.

Americans Talk Issues. *The Emerging World Order*. Survey No. 16. Winchester, MA, July 1991.

Food and Agriculture Organization of the United Nations. *FAO Global Information and Early Warning System on Food and Agriculture*. Rome, Special Alert No. 223. July 22, 1991.

Middle East Watch. *A Victory Turned Sour: Human Rights in Kuwait Since Liberation*. Washington D.C., September 1991.

National Council of Churches. *Pressing for Peace*. New York, 1991.

U.S. General Accounting Office. *Cost of Operation Desert Shield and Desert Storm and Allied Contributions*. Testimony by Frank C.

Conahan before the Committee on the Budget, U.S. House of Representatives,Washington D.C., May 15, 1991.

-----. *Operation Desert Shield/Storm: Costs and Funding Requirements*. GAO/NSIAD-91-304, Washington D.C., September 1991.

Index

ABOUT THE AUTHOR

DENNIS MENOS is a research and management consultant and a writer on national security affairs. He formerly served at the Department of Defense in senior analyst and executive positions. He is the author of three books--*Arms Control Fact Book, World at Risk,* and *The Superpowers and Nuclear Arms Control* (Praeger, 1990).

DATE DUE		
OCT 2 0 1998		
MAR 13 1998		